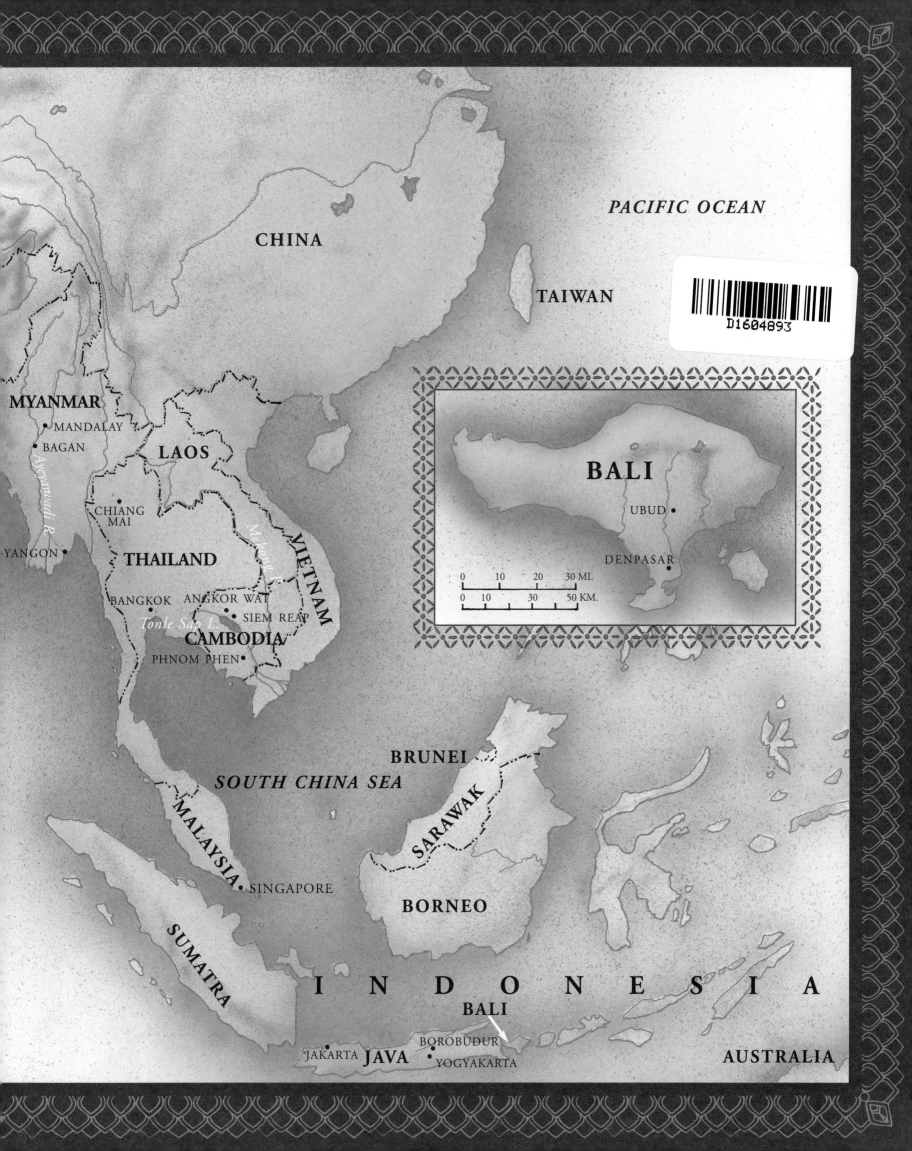

PACIFIC OCEAN

CHINA

TAIWAN

MYANMAR

MANDALAY

BAGAN

LAOS

*Ayeyarwadi R.*

CHIANG MAI

THAILAND

YANGON

*Mekong R.*

VIETNAM

BANGKOK

ANGKOR WAT

*Tonle Sap L.*

SIEM REAP

CAMBODIA

PHNOM PHEN

BALI

UBUD •

DENPASAR •

| 0 | 10 | 20 | 30 MI. |
| 0 | 10 | 30 | 50 KM. |

BRUNEI

SOUTH CHINA SEA

MALAYSIA

SARAWAK

• SINGAPORE

BORNEO

SUMATRA

I N D O N E S I A

BALI

BOROBUDUR

JAKARTA • JAVA • YOGYAKARTA

AUSTRALIA

# Sacred Places of Asia

WHERE EVERY BREATH IS A PRAYER

# Sacred Places of Asia

## WHERE EVERY BREATH IS A PRAYER

JON ORTNER

ABBEVILLE PRESS PUBLISHERS

NEW YORK • LONDON • PARIS

# CONTENTS

Horseman crossing the Kali Gandaki River, Nepal

Dhaulagiri Peak with glacier, in the Kali Gandaki Gorge, Nepal

# FOREWORD

Our planet has rarely, if ever, been so assaulted by a single species. Chemicals tear the envelope above us that allows life to thrive. Forests teeming with the diversity of life fall daily to the relentless march of a human population growing without restriction. Abused top soil is lost forever to the wind. Even its image has suffered, as we rush to shrink the continents to the size of shops in a global bazaar. How comforting to know there is still a place on earth where the beauty and mystery of the natural world is so inspiring it defies even the technological culture of the late twentieth century.

Millennia ago, the same mists swirling about the stone spires of the Himalaya sent holy men on unending journeys searching for spiritual meaning among the sacred heights. Even the Hindu prince Siddhartha Gautama threw off his comfortable surroundings to embark on a lifelong journey toward Buddhist enlightenment in these mountains. We're fortunate that Jon Ortner joined their timeless pilgrimage and allows us now to share the magnificent views of unchanged traditions throughout this spectacular landscape.

By looking at the spiritual heart of the world's most mysterious region, Ortner reveals some lessons that are curiously contemporary. Through modern science and technology, we seek to dominate nature and ultimately control it. These images remind us that ancient cultures regarded their landscape with mystical, sacred respect and shaped their beliefs accordingly. Harmony and synchronization with the cycles of the natural world were most important to them and they evolved as an integral part of nature, not as an opposition to it.

Jon Ortner's mountains seem to touch the sky, soaring above a land that is understandably filled with creation myths and legends. The Ganges River in India is revered as the most holy place on earth for Hindus. The photographs here allow us to appreciate Varanasi, the City of Shiva, as a pilgrimage place used for countless centuries and the spiritual focal point on every Hindu's path to Nirvana. Angkor Wat slept hidden in the Cambodian jungle, yet we learn that it is still a place of Buddhist pilgrimage and the largest religious building in the world. We see the evolution of Buddhism and Hinduism throughout Asia and the adaptation of these awakened teachings to the land and its people.

We pierce the veil of time and distance to view another way of life. And what may be visually shocking at first, ultimately presents us with a rare glimpse into the most ancient and important philosophical concepts of mankind. Be prepared for more than a remarkable odyssey through time-worn holy places. By focusing on these haunting images of the spirit world, Jon Ortner suggests a course for our future.

The wonders found among the peaks and architectural treasures reveal the deep respect these cultures hold for what nature provides; a reverence toward the life-giving source of food, water, and shelter and a deep understanding of the natural world as being a gift to mankind, to be respected, cared for, and exalted. We can learn from that.

Call it an "enlightened" view of the world around us.

BILL KURTIS, April, 1996

*Bill Kurtis, journalist and author of*
Bill Kurtis on Assignment,
*is the executive producer and host of* The New Explorers,
*as well as* Investigative Reports *and* American Justice
*on the A&E television networks.*

# PREFACE

Early one cold, grey, and misty morning in the middle of February, I was called urgently to the Vishnu Paduka temple in Gorkana, as the auspicious moment of rededication had arrived—the blessing and anointment of the stone on which the religious beliefs and indeed the structure itself would depend. We had waited days for this propitious hour, and the simple yet poignant ceremony that took place at the bottom of a deep, dark pit still flashes through my mind—the colors of vermilion powder, yellow marigolds, white yogurt, and the amber glow of oil—all mingled with the incense and the waters of the four oceans that were used to complete the consecration of the site. Although I had arrived in the country many years before as a young conservation architect charged with the task of renovating one of the largest monument complexes in the Kathmandu Valley, such imagery will be forever in my mind as I am certain that this ceremony was my induction into the vocation of temple conservation.

For those of you who have never had the chance to experience the mysticism of the East or to be transported into another world, far from your own base camp, you will see through photographer Jon Ortner's lens, a very individual set of experiences that I am sure, will inspire you to a new depth of understanding. For those of you who have been fortunate to have travelled to even one of these special sites, this book will evoke memories from within that you would not believe were there.

The names of the destinations alone—Kathmandu, Angkor, Borobudur, and Ladakh—cannot fail to evoke in the minds of all travellers the very essence of Asia. Its intense colour, its devotion, its perfume characterise a quality of life very different to that found in the West.

In these places, there is an understanding of life and death, and a mindfulness of nature. For me this intensity has been heightened due to my long association with the monuments and places in Asia. Because I have had the good fortune of becoming more than a fleeting visitor, I have embraced the opportunities of discovery—cutting paths through the dense jungles of Angkor to happen upon a temple complex such as Preah Khan, and to plan and implement its renaissance as a romantic ruin. I have accepted the challenge of reviving the Newari building crafts of the Kathmandu Valley to renovate the Hanuman Dhoka Royal Palace—a masterpiece of the traditional skills of the Malla dynasty in the centre of Kathmandu. I have suffered the senses of despair and jubilation in fighting to save the environment of Swayambhu—the original lotus floating on the lake that formerly filled the Kathmandu Valley—against the surge of "westernization."

These experiences have given me a chance to observe the great monuments of Asia from a more acute angle and it is with great delight that I contemplate the images of Jon Ortner as he has truly captured a sense of depth; a sense of beauty that I also behold in these sites—the serenity of Bagan, the majesty of Ladakh, the magnitude of Angkor—all of which are linked with a mantra, or prayer.

In *Where Every Breath is a Prayer*, Jon Ortner certainly has been able to distill my reflections of Asia and I have enjoyed experiencing his perceptions as he took me to each of these remarkable destinations where architecture and religion are inseparable. I am sure that those of you who know Asia already and are joining Jon on his pilgrimage will experience his sense of religious intensity at each site and will relive their own past experiences of Asia. For those who have yet to experience Asia and its variety of moods, here is a unique introduction.

JOHN SANDAY, March, 1996

*John Sanday, the author of the*
Collins Illustrated Guide to the Kathmandu Valley,
*is a preservation consultant and an advisor for
the World Monuments Fund.*

Trading caravan crossing the Kali Gandaki River, Nepal

Village of Jhong in a side valley of the Kali Gandaki Gorge, Nepal

# INTRODUCTION

*"Have you also learned that secret from the river; that there is no such
thing as time? . . . the river is everywhere at the same time, at the source
and at the mouth, at the waterfall, at the ferry, at the current, in the
ocean and in the mountains, everywhere, and . . . the present only exists
for it, not the shadow of the past, nor the shadow of the future."*

It was these words from the story of *Siddhartha* by Herman Hesse, that first sparked my interest in Asia. Like a tiny seed in my soul, the desire to journey to the mystical Land of the East grew into a burning passion.

In 1970, fresh out of high school, I left with a friend for my first trip to India, Nepal, and the Himalaya. After touring the subcontinent for a month, we found our way to a paradise known as the Vale of Kashmir. Nestled between India and Pakistan, perched among the highest mountains in the world, Kashmir remains one of the most beautiful valleys in the Himalaya.

While staying in a houseboat among the waterlilies of Dal Lake, I first heard of the holy cave of Amarnath. For thousands of years, it has been a pilgrimage site for Shiva *sadhus*. These Hindu holy men, along with tens of thousands of worshipers, gather at the cave each year during the full moon of *sawan* in high summer. They come to revere a magical object that symbolizes the phallus, or *lingam*, of Shiva. The cave itself is hidden among the icy peaks of the high Himalaya and required four days of rugged hiking to reach. At the back wall of the towering cavern is the amazing focus of *sadhus'* veneration: an enormous ice stalagmite said to miraculously grow and shrink with the waxing and waning of the moon.

I was determined to experience the magic first hand, and so my friend and I set off with our porter, Rajbar, to begin our first trek into the legendary Himalaya. I was unprepared—not just for the cold and the altitude—but also for the overpow-

Ice *lingam* in the cave at Amarnath.

ering beauty of these holy mountains. Only now do I realize the effect this first journey would have upon the rest of my life.

Each night we sheltered in communal tents with groups of ocher-robed ascetics. Our conversations lasted through the star-filled nights and included intense discussions of Hindu philosophy, the effects of karma, and the inevitability of sickness, death, and reincarnation. These *sannyasis,* or seekers, spoke of the superhuman powers of yogic concentration and of the great holy places that each of them had visited during years of unwavering devotion. Their ritual journeys had led them throughout India and along the most remote trails of the Himalaya. Each night we drifted off to sleep with our minds filled with tales of wandering seers and each morning we awoke to find ourselves in the overwhelming presence of the most majestic mountains on earth.

The *sadhus* also spoke to us of the Mahaparikrama, or the Great Pilgrimage Circuit, an immense physical and spiritual journey covering thousands of miles and requiring sixty years or more to complete. Many of the five million Shiva ascetics begin their life of pilgrimage at Kanya Kumari, at the southern tip of India. In a grand clockwise migration, these mendicants walk from shrine to shrine, many virtually naked, carrying few possessions. At each of their stops, they pay homage to Shiva through incense burning, meditative prayers, and yogic excercises. They continue to make their way north to Muktinath and Pashupati in Nepal, to the source of the Ganges, then on to Amarnath Cave, and finally to Kailash, a remote peak in western Tibet. This is the most sacred place of all, recognized by both Hindus and Buddhists as the center of the universe.

When I finally arrived at the cave, the icy *lingam*—symbol of Shiva's creative power—was covered with flower petals and surrounded with incense. It was lovingly tended to by a group of kind and generous holy men, many of them yogic masters who had spent the entire winter meditating there with little food and even less warmth. It was these gentle yogis, dressed in mere slips of cloth, who first made me feel so comfortable and so at home in such an utterly foreign place.

After returning to America, my interest in Asian pilgrimage and the ascetic ideals of Hinduism and Buddhism continued to grow. I became increasingly fascinated with this ancient tradition and the concept of sacred topography. These ascetics, unencumbered by ego or possessions, were participants in a timeless quest for enlightenment, a search for something to which many people, including myself, were inexplicably drawn. I know now that it was there and then—at Amarnath—that this book began to take shape.

My experiences at Amarnath led me on to many other locations of great antiquity and spiritual power, such as the Indonesian island of Bali. As at Amarnath, I was greatly impressed by its continuation of timeless rituals and devotion to the spiritual world. One night, while watching a performance of the Semara Rathi Dance Troupe in Ubud, I truly felt that I had again entered a world where ritual was used to connect the individual soul with the divine cosmos. The experience was extraordinary: exquisite young dancers were wrapped tightly in colored silk brocades and gold printed sashes and crowned with fragrant plumeria flower headdresses. With the light from oil lamps sparkling and reflecting off of their bodies, they spun and twirled to the complex syncopation of a gamelan orchestra. Sweat glistened and ran down their faces; visions of ecstasy flashed across their eyes. They became celestial dancers, birds of paradise enrapt in a spiritual trance fueled by communion with divine powers.

This is my *puja*: an offering of my deepest respect and love for the people, the philosophies, and the sacred places of Asia. It is the visual essence of my experiences throughout twenty years of pilgrimage; a pilgrimage that began with the trek to Amarnath Cave, led to adventures throughout Kashmir, Ladakh, Nepal, and ultimately widened to include Thailand, Myanmar, Cambodia, Java, and Bali. At all of these locations I looked for a primordial spiritual resonance that was both visible and tangible. These images depict the symbolic poetry of ritual, gesture, time and place. They are a personal vision of the spiritual worlds of which I have been privileged to be a part. In these portraits the dancers, no less than the yogis, transcend their physical existence and cross a bridge from the mundane world to the enlightenment of spiritual world. And for a brief time they exist in that place "where every breath is a prayer."

JON ORTNER, March, 1996

# NEPAL HIMALAYA

Fallen flowers from a simal, or silk cotton tree (*Salmalia malabaricum*).

Sixty-five million years ago, the collision of two great prehistoric continents created the highest mountains in the world, the mighty Himalaya—a mosaic of enormous peaks, sinuous glaciers, extensive high-altitude plateaus, and plunging valleys. Pushed by titanic forces from the bottom of the Tethys Sea, this spectacular mountain range is over fifteen hundred miles long and more than one hundred and fifty miles wide, and features a vast network of parallel groups of peaks, or *himals,* that spans the countries of Afghanistan, Pakistan, India, Nepal, China, Bhutan, and Myanmar. Of its peaks, fourteen rise above 26,240 feet (known to mountaineers as the "eight-thousand-meter peaks"), and more than four hundred are higher than 22,960 feet, ("seven-thousand-meter peaks"), making the Himalaya the greatest concentration of high mountains in the world.

In shaping these youngest and most rapidly growing of earth's mountains, tectonic forces have created an isolated world of environmental extremes. Dense tropical jungle and arctic ice fields share the same mountain slopes. From barren, windswept heights to ancient, moss-draped climax forests of rhododendron, fir, and spruce, the geographic and biological wonders of the Himalaya have yet to be fully cataloged, and substantial portions of this immense mountain kingdom remain unmapped and unexplored.

Separating the Occidental civilization of Mesopotamia and the Oriental cultures of Southeast Asia, the Himalaya became a crossroads of the world's great early cultures and a melting pot for the fusion of Eurasian races. Paleolithic wanderers followed trails and animal paths used by earlier hunter-gatherers. In their quest for survival, they were led deep into the forbidding Himalayan wilderness and there discovered a mountain world of untapped resources and extraordinary natural wonders. These migrants must have been inspired by the overwhelming scale and surreal beauty of the surrounding landscape, for it became the critical factor in the evolution of man's earliest spiritual traditions. In fact, the indigenous, animistic beliefs founded in the Himalaya formed the basis of the oldest, continuously practiced religious rituals on the planet.

Animism, the belief that spirits reside in nature, flourished in the Himalaya long before recorded history. Worship began with the first shamans and ascetics who established sacred sites along holy rivers and throughout the Himalaya Mountains. Aided by their encounters with soma, an intoxicating extract from a psychoactive plant, these holy men communed with nature spirits—the deities living in the peaks, rivers, and forests. Seeking *mauneya unmada,* or *munis* intoxication, these first seers would enter an ecstatic trance state that sensitized and aligned them to the invisible energies emanating from the holy sites.

Migration into the Himalaya continued with the diverse ethnic groups that followed the paths forged by the early shamans and ascetics. Though perhaps seeking alternate trade routes, they must have also been strongly attracted to, and profoundly affected by, the spirituality of the region. With the passage of time, places of spiritual resonance became highly venerated and an intricate sacred topography began to evolve. A vast mandala was created—a holy diagram of invisible lines connecting holy sites— that projected the energies of the gods over the expanse of the Himalaya, the Gangetic Plains, and the Tibetan Plateau.

Holy areas of the Himalaya were often characterized by exceptional physical beauty. Charged with spiritual power, they acted as symbolic portals to the world of

sacred understanding. Imposing mountain peaks were seen as the pristine celestial homes of the gods, and caves were believed to be the entrances to the primordial womb of Mother Earth. Deep in protective forests, the still waters of ponds and lakes were home to *autochthonous* deities—indigenous spirits which sprang spontaneously from the landscape. Crystalline rivers rushing down from peaks were offspring of the gods and symbols of enlightenment that purified and nourished everything in their path.

The attachment of spiritual significance to water prompted the genesis of pilgrimage, which based itself on *thirta yatra,* the physical act of fording a river or stream or traveling to a sacred confluence of water known as a *prayag. Prayag*s were considered holy seats of the gods, and visiting them became the goal of pilgrims and holy men who were searching to understand the great mysteries of the universe.

It was this mystical union between the mortal seeker and the primordial powers of nature that gave rise to the two great meditative religions of Hinduism and Buddhism.

The Dudh Kosi Gorge is the entrance to Khumbu Nepal, which is the homeland of the Sherpas, an eastern Tibetan tribe that migrated to the Everest area approximately six hundred years ago.

PAGES 24–25: In the shadow of Everest, Lhotse, the fourth highest mountain in the world at 27,923 feet, features strata of limestone and crystalline rock.

RIGHT: Ama Dablan, as seen from the Thyangboche monastery at an altitude of 12,700 feet. Housing thirty-five monks of the Tibetan Buddhist Nyingmapa Order, Thyangboche takes its name from Thyan, meaning "great high place," and is a cultural and religious center for Sherpas.

PAGES 28–29: The Gurung village of Gandrung, Nepal, with the Annapurna Sanctuary in the background.

PAGE 29 *top*: The eastern Himalaya boast the greatest varieties and most extensive forests of rhododendron in the world. This rhododendron forest canopies the trail to the Annapurna Sanctuary.

## ANNAPURNA SANCTUARY

Up from the steaming, tropical lowlands in central Nepal, rises the magnificent Annapurna Range. A wall of rock and ice-clad summits forty miles long, it is comprised of hundreds of serrated peaks—sixteen of which are higher than twenty thousand feet—and is cradled by rivers that make up its eastern and western boundaries. Sisters in grandeur, they have each created two of the deepest gorges in the world: the Kali Gandaki on the west and the Marsyandi Khola on the east. Unfathomably deep, their chasms are more than three times the depth of Colorado's Grand Canyon.

This complement of extreme of height and depth between mountain and gorge is responsible for the unusual duality of climate found in the Annapurna range. Its southern-facing slopes are covered in dense tropical jungles of rhododendron and bamboo, while its northern faces are in rain shadow, with a drier, colder climate similar to that of the nearby Tibetan Plateau.

Living near such inspiring topography, the ancient people of the surrounding lowlands worshiped the range, naming it after the Hindu goddess Annapurna, the giver of bounty and provider of food. Of those tribes that made it their home, it was the Gurungs, an ancient Nepalese people, who ultimately migrated deep into the mountain range and found their way through the jungle to the incredible, almost impenetrable, heart of the *himal*—the hidden preserve of the Annapurna Sanctuary.

The sanctuary is an enormous cirque, or alpine basin, situated at an elevation of fourteen thousand feet. Surrounded by nine Himalayan giants, this three-mile-wide oval ampitheater receives only seven hours of sunlight a day. It is an otherwise unremarkable landscape—a gently rolling meadow of grass and moraine—but against massive curtains of ice and snow, it is truly remarkable. To stand on this high-altitude plateau

Threat of avalanche is always present in the narrow Modi
Khola Gorge, the gateway to the sanctuary.

RIGHT: The Annapurna Sanctuary with the peaks of Annapurna
South on the left and Annapurna I on the right

and to look up is to be overwhelmed by the sheer vertical walls of
rock that bound it: Annapurna South, at 23,607 feet;
Machapuchare at 22,942 feet; and the tenth highest peak on earth,
Annapurna I, at an astounding 26,545 feet. The glaciers of these
peaks are the source of Modi Khola River that drains the sanctuary
through a narrow opening in its precipitous southern wall.

This opening is the only way in or out of the sanctuary, and
the Gurungs believe that this "secret" path through the Modi Khola
Gorge was protected by their god Pujinim Barahar, who had to be
propitiated before anyone could safely enter the sacred grounds of
the sanctuary. Machapuchare, the crystalline peak that guards the
entrance, was said to be the home of Shiva, and its snow plumes
were believed to be the smoke of his heavenly incense.

Sadly, the number of trekkers and expeditions visiting the
sanctuary has increased dramatically in recent years, and litter, the
indiscriminate cutting of trees, and trail erosion have threatened its
delicate ecological balance. In response to this damaging overuse,
the Annapurna Sanctuary became part of the larger Annapurna
Conservation Area in 1986. The resulting restrictions placed on the
number of trekkers, the use of firewood, and grazing by animals
could allow the sanctuary to heal and may inspire the public to
honor it with the same respect and reverence the Gurung still hold
in their worship of it.

OPPOSITE: A small tea station by a trail near the lower Marsyandi River.

These young Gurung girls are the direct descendants of the first tribe to forge the early path through the tenacious Modi Khola Gorge.

The Duna Khola drains the vertiginous western face of Manaslu. Only a few expeditions have traveled to these remote and treacherous "mountains of the mind."

OPPOSITE TOP: The village of Naje and surrounding fields high above the Marsyandi River.

OPPOSITE BOTTOM: Usnea moss, an epiphytic air plant, drapes the birch and bamboo forest of the upper Duna Khola.

34

The steep slopes and frequent avalanches
of the Marsyandi Gorge prevent any
forest variety but bamboo to flourish.

Buddhist prayer flags decorate the slate
roofs of houses in upper Pisang in the
Manang Valley of central Nepal. Hundreds
of devotional prayers printed on cloth are
directed to the heavens.

PAGES 38–39: The fluted curtains of ice of the Grand
Barrier are the result of heavy snowfall and continuous avalanches. Over twenty-one thousand feet high
and eight miles long, it is one of the world's largest
ice walls.

# KALI GANDAKI GORGE

Placed at the threshold of a home in the Nepali village of Kag, a spirit catcher offers protection from evil spirits.

In a remote area of the Nepal Himalaya, there exists a gorge so deeply carved into the earth, it is visible from space. It is the Kali Gandaki, and at three-and-a-half times the depth of Colorado's Grand Canyon, it is the deepest gorge in the world. Formed by the Kali Gandaki River, this great cleft completely traverses the Himalayan Barrier, stretching from the high-altitude desert of the Tibetan steppe down to the tropical plains of India.

One of the most spectacular points in the Kali Gandaki Gorge is near the village of Dana, where the Kali Gandaki River snakes past Annapurna (26,795 feet) and Dhaulagiri (26,545 feet). Here, the mountain summits are only twenty-two miles apart, creating an immense chasm with walls over four miles high. These peaks are so tall that they actually pierce the jet stream, creating their own weather systems, and so massive that they block the advance of the annual monsoon and rob it of its moisture.

The geological extremes of the gorge have allowed a variety of natural ecosystems to evolve. Perhaps nowhere else in the world can one find climatic extremes compressed so spectacularly; tropical, arctic, and desert conditions are all found within a few miles

of each other and exhibit an unusual diversity of plant and animal life.

The location of the Kali Gandaki River is one of the reasons the Kali region, once called the Kingdom of Thak, supports such an ethnically diverse population. Because it was a natural trade route connecting central Asia with the Indian subcontinent, many races and cultures settled along it, including the Thakalis, the Gurungs, and the Bhotia—all of whom now peacefully coexist. They have been using this trans-Himalayan caravan route since man first migrated from the central Asian plateau. A vast system of timeworn trails connects ancient citadels along the river and is used to bring salt down from the high lakes of Tibet, by yak and donkey, to the lower Kali, to be traded for grain and other staples. The tax received on this trading funded the building of medieval fortresses as well as many fine Buddhist monasteries and temples, and provided the means by which Hindu and Buddhist communities could flourish.

The Kali Basin is also an important repository of Hindu and Buddhist religious culture. Numerous temples, as well as important prehistoric pilgrimage sites, are scattered throughout it. One of the most remarkable of its Hindu shrines is the Cave of the

The medieval fortress of Jharkot is home to the Tibetan-Buddhist Thakali Tribe. Behind it can be seen the peaks of the remote Dolpo region.

PAGES 42–43: Appearing as specks against the immense wall of the Kali Gorge, a woman and her child prepare a field for planting.

Orange lichen coats mani stones carved and made
sacred with the mantra, "Om Mani Padme Hum,"
meaning "Om the Jewel Within the Lotus."

Burning Waters, or Muktinath, at twelve thousand feet in the
Jhong Khola Valley. Inside the cave is a geological wonder: a
pairing of bubbling spring and natural gas flames, both emerg-
ing from the same subterranean chamber. It is unknown how
long the blue flames have danced with the holy water, but this
miraculous sight has attracted Hindu ascetics for many thousands of years.

The Cave of the Burning Waters is only one example
of the mysteries that still exist in the Kali Gandaki Gorge.
Nepal's xenophobia and local political stress along its sensitive
border with Chinese-occupied Tibet have kept the gorge rela-
tively unknown. Even today, some distant portions of the Kali
are uncharted and unexplored. (Incredibly, the source of the
Kali River was not discovered until 1966, when it was found
near the border of Tibet, in the distant kingdom of Mustang.)

Eventually, a road will be built through the gorge, connecting India with China. But for now, the Kali is a rugged
land of untouched Himalayan villages, pristine peaks, and geo-
logic wonders, one of the most unusual places in the world.

Across the Kali Gandaki Gorge, Dhaulagiri
Himal, the world's sixth highest peak, rises
above the villages of Khobang and Larjung.

# KATHMANDU VALLEY

Seen from Nagarjun Peak, this royally protected forest stands at the edge of the Kathmandu Valley.

Although the elliptical valley of Kathmandu takes up but a small portion of Nepal, it has been the cultural and political core of the nation throughout its history. Surrounded by the highest and most revered mountains in the world, it was almost preordained that the valley would develop a complex sacred topography. Nowhere else can the sanctity and reverence for a land be better witnessed than by the presence of the thousands of ancient shrines, architectural monuments, and religious wonders that dot its hilltops and riversides, and lay sequestered deep within its dark forests.

The successive waves of peoples and philosophies that influenced Kathmandu made it a true meeting place of Hindu and Buddhist worlds. The country of Nepal was the crucible in which more than thirty tribes, each with its own distinct religious culture, forged a remarkably homogeneous and refined civilization. Here, the animistic traditions of the prehistoric Himalaya merged with the sophistication of Hindu and Buddhist thought. Propelled by the artistic and philosophical genius of the Newars—a race that first settled the valley over three thousand years ago—a Tantric Hindu tradition evolved in Kathmandu that included aspects of both orthodox Hindu schools, such as Samkya Yoga, and the highly complex metaphysical world of Vajrayana Buddhism.

A critical factor in the development of this tradition was the extreme fertility of the valley's alluvial soil. The inhabitants of Kathmandu were able to grow three rice harvests a year and maintain prodigious stores of fruits and vegetables. This surplus of food enabled the people to develop a highly evolved spiritual and commercial kingdom as early as 700 B.C. Diaries of Chinese pilgrims found in A.D. 700 describe the Kathmandu Valley as a place filled with prosperous towns, lavish palaces, and temples crowned with spires of gold.

Pilgrims and sages have been compelled to come to Kathmandu for millennia. Among some of its oldest-known pilgrims are Shiva *sadhus* and Siddhartha Gautama Buddha, who taught in the hillside forest that surrounds Swayambhu. Over thousands of years a widespread geographic network of sacred places has evolved—a geometric arrangement of shrines formed in the shape of a huge mandala, or circular meditation symbol. The three largest of these shrines—Pashupati, Swayambhu, and Baudha— remain among the most important and remarkable temples in the Himalaya, with historical roots going back well before the birth of the Buddha. These, along with hundreds of other sites continue to draw pilgrims and ascetics from the far corners of Asia.

A view across the Kathmandu Valley to the High Himalaya.

PAGES 50–51: Newari homes dot the verdant terraces of the Mahabarat Range at the edge of the Kathmandu Valley.

A *sadhu* stands before a self-emanated *lingam* in a Pashupati field that has been sanctified by its presence.

Kathmandu is a dramatic place where art, religion, and worship of the land are inextricably interwoven. The mountains that surround it are still believed to be populated by gods and spirits who rule all aspects of Nepali life from birth to death. Each town and village has its own patron deity and the valley contains temples devoted to almost every divinity in the Hindu and Buddhist pantheons. Even the politics of Nepal—the world's last Hindu kingdom—are controlled by the deities, and its current king, Birendra Bir Bikram Shah Dev, is worshiped as a living, human incarnation of the Hindu god Vishnu.

What is so remarkable about the evolution of the Kathmandu Valley is the rare synthesis of cultures and religious thought that occurred here. But perhaps even more remarkable is the great achievement of the Newars and other Nepali tribes in retaining the sanctity of the land—a preservation guaranteed by the continual homage, through ritual, to a wisdom stretching back to the dawn of time.

# PASHUPATI

Countless centuries ago in the Himalayan kingdom of Nepal, a peasant farmer patiently tended his fields. As he worked, he watched a cow wander to the edge of a nearby forest. To his surprise, this most sacred of animals released her milk over a small earthen mound, where it seeped into the ground. When this strange behavior was repeated a few days later, the farmer dug down into the spot and found an astonishing object: here was a stone *lingam,* or carved phallus, and on the sides of the *lingam* were the four faces, or aspects, of Shiva, God of the Ascetics.

The Nepalese believe that this ancient stone column was self-emanated—not carved by the hand of man—and dates from a time when the cosmos was first manifested by the gods. Prophesied by legends and myths, this remarkable relic symbolizing the creative force of the universe is at the heart of Nepal's largest and most spectacular temple complex, Pashupati. On its hallowed grounds, Shiva is honored every day by thousands of rituals, culminating in Shiva Ratri (Shiva's Night), Nepal's largest religious festival. The medieval pageant draws hundreds of thousands of pilgrims, many of whom have walked from as far as southern India and Tibet to experience *darshan,* the sighting of the divine.

Pashupati encompasses a huge forested hill through which the sacred Bagmati River flows. Lining the banks of the river and scattered in the recesses of the fog-shrouded forest are hundreds of intricately carved temples, shrines, and religious objects

Delicate features mark the self-emanated face of Shiva's wife and consort, Gauri, known as The Shining One, in a rock configuration on a bank of the Bagmati River.

OPPOSITE: A wandering ascetic, or *sannyasi,* displays an advanced *asana,* or yogic position. He has dispelled all imperfections and is in a state of *avadhuta*—as is Shiva, The Divine Yogi, who is at all times perfectly controlled. The *sannyasi* is near naked, or *digambara,* meaning "sky-clad;" and he is covered with *vibhuti,* ash that represents Shiva's Dissolution of the Universe, the end of the eternal cosmic cycle.

RIGHT: Unusually young to be devoting her life to renunciation and discipline, this *sadhvi,* or female *sadhu,* wears the signs of Shiva. She is a *tapasa,* one who practices austerities, or self-inflicted suffering, to gain psychic powers and control over the physical body.

Two pilgrims meditate on the ghats of the Bagmati River at Pashupati in Kathmandu, Nepal. Ghats are stone platforms used for meditation, cremation, and other Hindu rituals.

OPPOSITE: Buried alive for three days, the hand of a *sadhu* is all that can be seen of his extreme penance. Known as *samadh,* it is one of the most severe of austerities and requires total yogic control of breathing and heart rate.

PAGES 58–59: The Rajarajeshvari Ghat is reflected in the Bagmati River in Pashupati, Nepal.

that are dedicated to Shiva and other gods of the Hindu pantheon. Ancient trees shade stone pathways that wind from one moss-covered shrine to another. Countless masterpieces in stone, some covered with gold, decorate the hillsides to form a unique living museum—a holy place yielding insight into the evolution of art, architecture, and religion in the Himalaya.

For centuries this location has resonated with a divine aura, embodying a mystical attraction as a dwelling place of deities and spirits, where religious energy has become focused and concentrated. Holy men and ascetics have congregated in the misty glades of Pashupati since before the time of Christ. These "living saints" circulate freely within the sacred landscape of pagodas, screeching monkeys, and pastel-robed pilgrims. Their presence, and the spectacle of yogis displaying inexplicable, superhuman powers, confirms and enhances Pashupati's importance.

Pashupati, a spiritual magnet and a center of traditional teaching, is fully integrated into the lives of the people of Nepal, and the essence of Lord Pashupati permeates every facet of existence. Throughout Nepal's history, Shiva incarnated as Pashupati has been venerated as the protector and patron deity of the country. Each morning, Radio Nepal begins its broadcast with a devotional song in his praise. He is figured into the Royal coat of arms, and it is only with Lord Pashupati's blessing that the King of Nepal may rule.

Pashupati is a microcosm of Hindu civilization where one can observe the entire spectrum of life from the sacred to the mundane. Women wash their clothes against the

An encampment of Vishnu ascetics in a *dharmsala,* a temple shelter where pilgrims can rest and receive food donations.

same stones from which the temples are built; they bathe daily in the same holy river that will finally carry their ashes away. In a larger sense, Pashupati symbolizes the entire sacred topography of the Indian subcontinent, with the Bagmati River as the Ganges, the forested hills as the Himalaya, and the temples as the great Hindu pilgrimage sites.

Pilgrims view Pashupati as a place of miracles, from the self-emanation of objects to the incredible mental and physical feats of holy men. The marvels that abound contradict Western notions of natural law and are thought to be due to divine intervention. Pashupati has always been a place where extraordinary events have occurred and, even today, remains a place where the supernatural seems natural.

These *lingam* shrines are found in the
Mrigasthali Forest, a part of the sacred grounds
and pilgrimage circuit of Pashupati. Each shrine
houses a votive *lingam,* and also displays a huge
bell and an egg-shaped *lingam* called an *anda.* A
ritual *puja,* or prayer, to one of these shrines
could include ringing the bell, making a rice
offering, dabbing the shrine with vermilion
powder, or anointing it lovingly with milk, butter, or holy water from the Bagmati River.

Each Hindu god possesses a *vahana,* or vehicle that represents the particular god's energy or character. For Shiva, it is the Nandi, a bull said to have been given to him by Brahma as a reward for settling a dispute.

OPPOSITE: Goat heads, dyed the color of sacrificial fire, await use in a Kali or Durga ceremony.

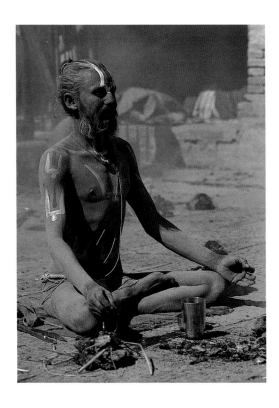

This Shiva *sadhu* is performing the Five Fire Austerity or Panch-Agni-Tapasya. This penance involves surrounding himself with four sacrificial fires and the symbolic fire of the sun. The smoke from smoldering cow dung purifies the temple courtyard. His fingers are in the Tyaga Mudra, the hand gesture symbolizing the renunciation of worldly things.

RIGHT: Pilgrims bathe for ritual purification at the Gauri Ghat on the Bagmati River in Pashupati.

*Sadhus* spread cow dung mixed with sacred Bagmati water upon the temple courtyard to purify it in preparation for meditation and yogic austerities. The *sadhu* in the center is wearing a chastity belt consisting of a metal waistchain, or *arbandh,* and a *langotis* cup.

PAGES 66–67: *Sadhus* paint their bodies with *tilaks,* the marks of Shiva. At least five *tilaks* should appear on the body, although thirty-two is the ideal number. The round *pindu,* the emblem of Shiva, is the Third Eye or Wisdom Eye. Among other meanings, the three horizontal lines across the forehead represent the three sources of light: the sun, the moon, and fire.

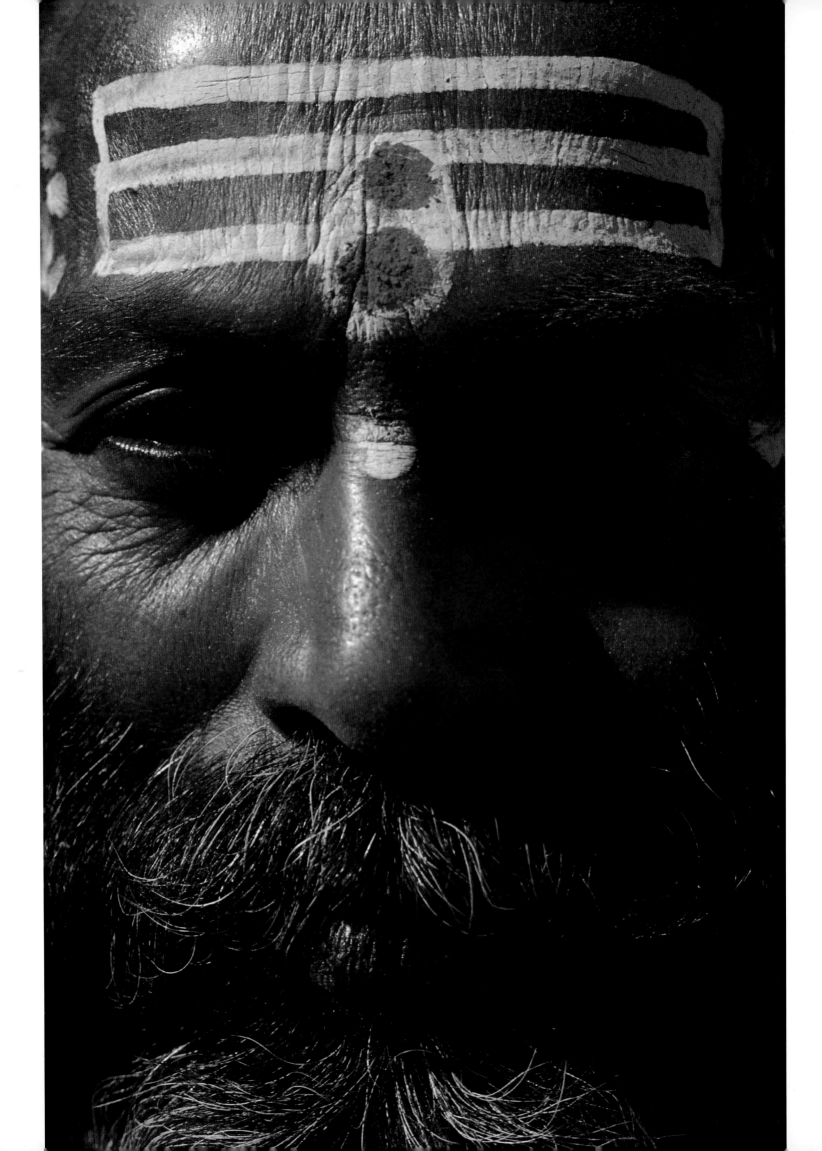

Two women wrapped against the chill of a
Kathmandu morning.

OPPOSITE: More than five million Shiva devotees
  follow the pilgrimage routes through India
  and the Himalaya; all carrying few possessions, some even traveling naked. Gracing
  the neck of this *sannyasi* is a *rudraksha*, or
  rosary of beads made from the seeds of the
  utrasum (*Elaeocarpus*) tree.

A 1686 sculpture of Maheshmardini from Bagwati Mandir presents one of the fearful aspects, or representations of the Mother Goddess, Durga. She is flanked by two images of the monkey-god Hanuman.

OPPOSITE: Built by Pratap Malla, the fourteenth-century Dakshinkali shrine is one of the most important in Nepal and is located on a *prayag* of two small streams. Seen here are the black stone images of Kali in two of her seven incarnations as Matrika. The copious amount of blood comes from live animal sacrifice, during which animal throats are slit and blood is squirted onto the sacred images.

All of these stone and metal representations of the tantric pantheon display the uncommon artistic skill of the Newars, the main tribe of the Kathmandu Valley.

Parvati, wife of Shiva.

OPPOSITE: *top left,* Lion at the Changu Narayan Temple; *top right,* A statue from the Annapurna Temple at Asan Tol depicts Chitipati carrying a bowl made from a human skull. He is helper to Kali at the cremation grounds; *bottom left,* A 1653 bronze and copper statue from the Uku Baha Temple in Patan; *bottom right,* An image of Hanuman at the Machhendranath Temple. He is a defender and assistant to the gods, and his legend is found in the Ramayana, one of the great epics of India.

Here, Shiva is in his *urdhvalinga* form. The erect penis symbolizes yogic control over sexuality and the achievement of *virtakas,* or a passionless state.

# SWAYAMBHU

Swayambhu, Nepal's most ancient shrine, seems to float like a sacred lotus on the cosmic ocean. Recent paleontological evidence suggests that the Kathmandu Valley was once the bottom of a massive prehistoric lake.

OPPOSITE: On a damp morning, two children play among votive stupas.

The key to understanding the sacredness of the Kathmandu Valley lies in its rich mythological history, as described through the legends found in an ancient text known as the Swayambhu Purana. First told by the Gautama Buddha, this story begins aeons ago during the golden age of the Krita Yuga—the beginning of the universe in its most perfect balance. It is said the valley was filled by an enormous aquamarine lake. Vastly deep and clear and surrounded by jungle-cloaked mountains, it was inhabited by a race of beings known as *nagas*, the "serpent deities of the Eight Directions." *Nagas* ruled supreme as the controlling deities of both the water and all the treasures beneath the earth. Named Nagavasahrada, or the Kingdom of the Nagas, this lake became the destination of a long lineage of wandering ascetics who sought to become "awakened ones."

One of the greatest of the holy men to arrive at Nagavasahrada was Vipaswi, an ascetic destined to be reborn as Sakyamuni, the historic Buddha of our era. Vipaswi threw a lotus root into the lake, where it bloomed into a flower of a thousand petals. Out from this blossom appeared a magnificent light that drew sages and pilgrims from throughout the Himalaya. They named this place Swayambhu, or The Self Created, and lived along its shore, devoting themselves to meditation and the worship of the *nagas* and the magical lotus.

The forest surrounding Manjushri Hill, where Gautama Buddha meditated with his followers. Like other ascetics, he was drawn to the sacred light of Swayambhu.

OPPOSITE: Close-up of the main *garbha*, the hemispherical dome or "womb," of the Swayambhu stupa. The stupa is maintained by the monks of the Tibetan Kagyupa Order and is believed to enclose the actual Jyotirupa, or "self-existent" light of Swayambhu. Partially visible are its thirteen gilt rings symbolizing the thirteen levels of perfection leading to nirvana, or enlightenment.

PAGES 78–79: Two Nepali men and their water buffalo rest at the base of a pipal, or fig tree. The Bodhi Tree under which Siddhartha Gautama Buddha became enlightened was also a pipal.

Eventually to Nagavasaharada came the Bodhisattva Manjushri, a Buddha dedicated to delaying his own enlightenment in order to help sentient beings. Manjushri saw that if the waters of the lake were drained, the pilgrims would be able to reach the shimmering light of Swayambhu directly. Once the *nagas* were properly appeased, Manjushri wielded his flaming sword of wisdom and cut deeply into the valley, causing the water to drain away. Thus the people were granted a sacred and fertile home in the Kathmandu Valley.

Today, the legacy of Swayambhu and the magical lotus is deeply intertwined with Hindu Tantric tradition. The Nepalese still annually worship the *nagas* and a shrine now stands at the site of the ancient lake. The lotus stem has grown through the earth, creating a cave that to this day remains unexplored, yet is believed to lead to the holy site of Pashupati. The lotus root was found at Pashupati, located on the Bagmati River, a Ganges tributary. It is between the shrines of Swayambhu and Pashupati, in the path of the lotus, that the city of wood and clay known as Kathmandu arose.

# BAUDHA

Inside the inner sanctum of Baudha, oil-lamp flames dance warmly against the silver-plated image of Chhwaskamini Ajima, a female Tibetan deity. In reverence, she is covered in brilliant, crushed vermilion, known as *puja* powder.

Located in the center of the Kathmandu Valley and surrounded by fifteen Tibetan monasteries, Baudha is the largest stupa, or Tibetan *chorten,* in Nepal. Built by King Manadev in the fifth century, it has been the city's most important Tibetan pilgrimage site since the thirteenth century.

The stupa rests on three, broad, square-shaped terraces that interlock to create a base that is *vimshatikona,* or "twenty-cornered." Encircling the *garbha* are 108 inlaid images of Amitabha, The Bodhisattva of the Unbounded Light.

On some stupas, especially those found in Nepal, the all-seeing eyes of Buddha are painted on each side of their steeples and represent the super-awareness of the enlightened mind. Here, the four aspects of the Buddha are presented as Akshobya Buddha, the symbol of mirror-like wisdom; Ratnasambhava Buddha, the symbol of equalizing wisdom; Amitablha Buddha, the symbol of discriminatory wisdom; and Amoghsidhi Buddha, the symbol of all-encompassing wisdom. The overall appearance is that of a giant Buddha sitting in meditative bliss, serenely looking out upon the material world. When viewed from above, the stupa appears as a circle, the symbol of completeness and total concentration of the mind. When seen from the side, the stupa is bell-shaped to remind pilgrims of the universal mantric ringing that will continue forever.

For Buddhists, the stupa shrine is the most ancient symbol of man's profound quest for higher consciousness, the search for Dharmadatu Jnan, or "the being as one with the universal spirit." Inspired by the shape of Mount Meru—the mythological center of the universe—it represents the abode of the gods on earth. It is a vehicle and an aid to the upward process of enlightenment and the god-like mind of Buddha.

Stupa architecture developed from an early belief that certain naturally occurring geometric shapes stored, generated, and amplified energy. This belief, held by many cultures, led to the primitive worship of monoliths and crystals, and later, as civilization evolved, to the construction of free-standing dolmans, tumuli, obelisks, and pyramids—all of which represent the unfathomable powers of nature.

The stupa began as a funereal monument, a reliquary in which the remains of great teachers and yogis were enshrined. These relics were regarded as precious seeds for future generations of devotees, providing the way by which any pilgrim could gain merit and achieve a spiritual oneness with the wisdom of the past.

The stupa receives and focuses mental energy. It is a generator that amplifies the spiritual fervor of a devotee and transmits it to the gods, while suffusing the entire area with an aura of sanctity. Through the act of ritual circumambulation—circling the stupa in a clockwise direction while repeating sacred mantra syllables—energy is created. Simple analogies would be winding a clock, charging a battery, or setting a wheel into motion. Circumambulation also reenacts The Turning of the Wheel of Dharma when the great truths were first revealed by Gautama Buddha.

The placement of stupas is critical. They are situated at the tops of mountain passes, along roads entering towns, and at other spots of telluric significance,

Baudha, in the Kathmandu Valley, Nepal.

PAGES 83–84: The diamond-studded, golden spire of Shwedagon at night, Yangon, Myanmar.

Swayambhu in the Kathmandu Valley, Nepal.

PAGES 85–86: Nakon Pathom, the largest stupa and the oldest Buddhist monument in Thailand, was constructed in the tenth century by the Mons—a Buddhist people from central Thailand—and restored to its present glory in 1853.

PAGES 88–89: Dressed in authentic brocade, jewelry, and hair adornment, Newari Tantric dancers from the Royal Institute for Nepali Sacred Arts perform at the entrance to the cave temple of Sekh Narayan. Trained rigorously in the art of Tantric dance, these young girls learn the *mudras,* or symbolic hand gestures, and the poses that tell the events in the lives of Buddhas and Bodhisattvas.

areas of strong magnetic currents; or geomantic significance, where underground forces combine with running water.

Architecturally, the stupa can be divided into five fundamental levels symbolizing the five basic elements of the universe: the square base denotes the earth; the second level is the hemispheric *garbha,* representing the womb and the infinite dome of sky from which all is emanated; the *harmika,* or cone, represents fire; the umbrella-shaped *hti,* is the insignia of air; and the curling finial, or *jyoti,* signifies the element of ether. The stupa is a guide to the evolution of the psyche and these five levels correspond to the ascending psychic energy centers, or *chakras,* of the human body.

Large stupas are entered through four directional portals, each of which depicts an important passage in the life of Buddha: the eastern entrance celebrates his birth; the southern marks his enlightenment; the western highlights his proclamation of the Dharma; and the northern represents his attainment of nirvana, or liberation.

The largest stupas in the world—Shwedagon, Borobudur, Nakhorn Pathom, and Baudha—are psychocosmograms, physical "maps" to enlightenment. When viewed from above, they appear as mandalas.

Used to protect against evil spirits, confer blessings, and purify all who circle it, the stupa is an architectural representation of the ultimate nature of reality; a key unlocking the door to the cosmological paradise of the gods, and ultimately, to nirvana.

# INDIA

Sunrise on Mother Ganga, the Ganges River in Varanasi, India.

## VARANASI

Along the western banks of India's Ganges River, at the site of what was once a prehistoric trade route, lies Varanasi, the oldest, continuously inhabited city in the world. Originally known as Kasi, City of Light—named for the thousands of golden temple spires seen from the river and for the luminous quality of its dawn light—Varanasi was already an ancient settlement when Siddhartha Gautama Buddha arrived around 500 B.C. Considered old, even by Asian standards, the city has witnessed the evolution of Indian civilization and is the most venerated spot on the entire fifteen hundred-mile course of the Ganges.

The very center of Hindu wisdom and enlightenment, Varanasi is alive in both the past and present. In addition to its great antiquity, it is one of the holiest cities in the world. There are no fewer than two thousand temples and one

A Bengali Shiva *sadhu*, on pilgrimage to the
Himalaya, performs the Masan Puja on the
bank of the Ganges, pouring sacred water
from his *kamandal,* or ritual water pot.

Sunrise marks the beginning of the Kartika
Purnima bathing festival at Asi Ghat. Kartika is
one of the three sacred months of bathing and
purification. Asi is a unique ghat because it has
remained a *kachcha,* or a ghat in its ancient,
stoneless, clay-bank form.

The grand celebration of Kartika Purnima continues, not only here at the Dasashvamedh Ghat, but at all the ghats on the Ganges. This river has attracted pilgrims and holy men from throughout Asia who follow in the steps of the ancient sages. The Ganges is a *prayag*, a holy confluence of the Varana, Asi, and Ganges Rivers, making it an exceptionally sacred site.

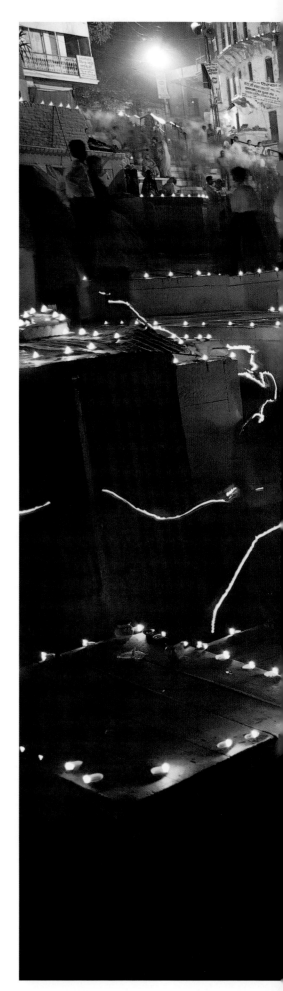

hundred thousand *lingams* hidden in its myriad winding alleyways. The entire precinct wherein the city lies is worshiped as a huge shrine to Shiva and it is here that the faithful come to reaffirm their relationship with god. Over seventy ghats—stone platforms with steps leading down into the Ganges—line four miles of riverbank. Ghats are used for meditation, prayer, and the ritual cleansing and purification that is the first obligation of every devout Hindu.

The Ganges River is the heart of Varanasi; she is Mother Ganga, emancipator and the remover of all afflictions. Varanasi is also the City of the Dead, the place of the ending of life. On the path to nirvana, all Hindus long to die on the Ganges. To do so guarantees the release of one's soul, an event called *moksha,* thus assuring liberation from *samsara,* the ceaseless cycle of birth, death, and reincarnation. The air by the riverside is hazy with the continuous smoke of some thirty-five thousand cremations performed each year on the Manikarnika and Harishchandra ghats. It is believed that for those who actually die on the banks of the river, a mantra is whispered into their ears by the god Shiva. This "mantra of the ferryboat crossing" is called the Taraka Mantra and guides the soul across the Ganges, through the passage between the world of the living and the sacred world of ancestors and gods.

Varanasi is one of the earth's central pilgrimage sites. Millions of devotees and yogis visit yearly, swelling the city's population of one and a half million, to as much as seven million during major festivals. It is as vital today as when the first Shiva ascetics came down from the Himalaya to established the oldest religion in the world. For twenty-five centuries, and through the eternal river Ganga, Varanasi has continued to inspire, purify, and rejuvenate all who come to her. Whether it is for death or rebirth, it is for all pilgrims the culmination of a lifetime of devotion.

ABOVE AND RIGHT: On the Panchganga Ghat during the nighttime continuation of the Kartika Purnima, a priest lights a ritual oil lamp that will join thousands of other small lamps sent floating down the Ganges on small leaf boats.

OPPOSITE: These followers from diverse Shiva sects have all come to the banks of the Ganges to continue the tradition of *tirtha yatra,* the merit of travel and the reverence for rivers that has gone on since the times of the early Vedic texts.

ABOVE: Hanuman is so highly revered by worshipers that when when a monkey dies, its body is ornately dressed, placed upon a throne, decorated with flowers and offerings, then ceremoniously carried and released into the Ganges River.

RIGHT: This meditating yogi is in the Sirsh Asana position. The sacred mud covering him has made its way down from the Himalaya and has been purified through the holy water of the Ganges.

LEFT AND ABOVE: Although the Ganges is
filled with sewage, disease-carrying
organisms, and the remains of incom-
plete cremations, pilgrims steadfastly
regard its water as undefileable and
bathe and drink from it freely. Purified
through ritual, holy Ganges water is
often brought back to individual
homes throughout India.

PAGES 100–101: Women bathe off of the
ritually decorated steps of Kedar Ghat, a
religious focal point of southern Varanasi.

PAGE 101: Surrounded by thousands yet soli-
tary in prayer, a woman seeks to wash
away her sins. A few devotees are so
drawn to the Ganges that they have spent
the latter part of their lives living and
praying at a single ghat from which they
never leave until death.

Attending the Kartika Purnima was one of my most memorable events in Varanasi. I had engaged my boatman, Ravi, to take me to the ancient, clay bank of Asi Ghat, one of the oldest spots on the Ganges River.

As we neared the shore, a thin veil of blue smoke rising from burning incense and nearby cremations drifted over a medieval scene. I was overwhelmed by the blaze of vibrant colors, the rich orchestration of sounds, and the mass of humanity before me: pilgrims bathing, praying, and chanting in exultation; saffron-robed *sadhus* seated on the ghat, blissfully repeating their holy mantras; a Brahman priest reading aloud from his sacred texts and dispensing blessings; a woman sitting on a woven mat, displaying her king cobra and seeking alms.

The sanctity and reverence of the moment enveloped me and I no longer wanted merely to observe. Stepping off the boat, I unconsciously accepted the help of an outstretched hand and allowed myself to be absorbed into the bewildering throng. As I looked about, I was greeted with smiles and nods from all directions. I felt privileged for I was accepted, even welcomed. It was understood we had all come to Mother Ganga for the same reason: to experience a communion with her, and with the timeless connection to the divinity that she represented.

The Agori *sadhus* are an ancient sect of shamanistic
holy men who officiate at the never-ending funerals.
Belonging to the most extreme of ascetic orders,
they are allowed to transgress all of society's rules
and behave with what is accepted to be a "divine
madness." They wear crystal rosaries called *sphatika,*
live near cemetaries and cremation grounds, collect
their food in human skulls, and cook their meals on
the cremation pyres.

RIGHT: Thirty-five thousand bodies are burned yearly at
the Manikarnika Ghat, said to be the final resting
place of all corpses upon the Dissolution of the
Universe. The Manikarnika Ghat is presided over by
the Doms, a literally untouchable caste. Although
they are wealthy concessioners who have controlled
the cremation firewood for thousands of years, they
are associated with the defilement of the ghat by
corpses and are physically touched by no Brahmin.

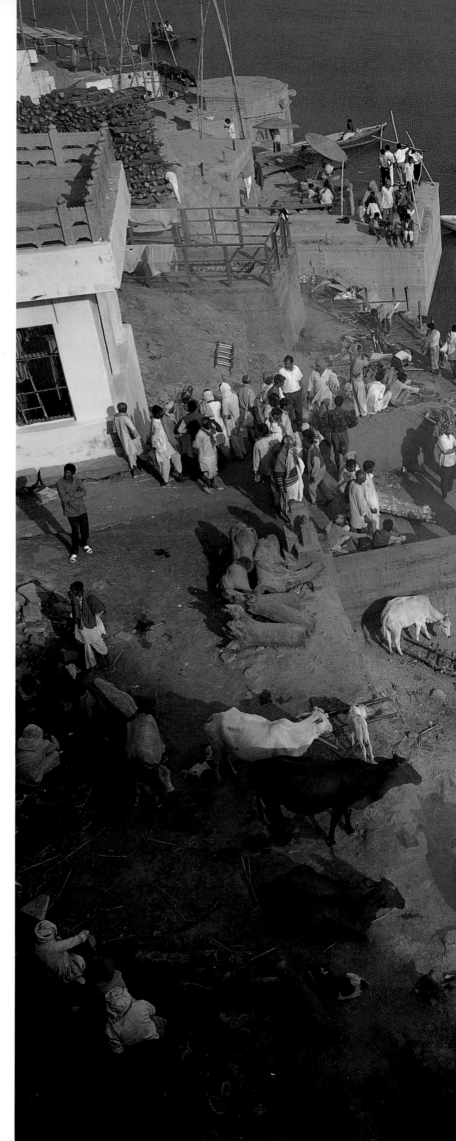

Dhamek, decorated in botanical reliefs, was built in A.D. 500 on the remains of another stupa from 200 B.C. It commemorates Gautama Buddha's first sermon during which he presented the Dharma: the Buddhist philosophy and world view that is made up of the Four Noble Truths and the Eight-Fold Path. The Wheel of the Dharma was turned during the sermon and symbolically marked the actual beginning of Buddhism.

# SARNATH

In 624 B.C., Siddhartha Gautama was born to the Shakya clan of Lumbini, a small town in Nepal. Brought up in an aristocratic family, he lived the first part of his life behind the sheltering walls of his father's palace, completely shielded from the harsh realities of the outside world; poverty, sickness, old age, and death were unknown to him. When finally exposed to these inevitabilities, he became deeply affected, then perplexed by the purpose of life. In response, he did what many ascetics, both Jain and Hindu, had done before him: he renounced the world of ego with all of its attachments and embarked upon a quest for the ultimate truth. Like other *sannyasis,* or seekers, he used yogic meditative techniques of mind and body control, practicing extreme physical and mental austerities to reach what is known as enlightenment, the perfect state of mind.

Siddhartha Gautama wandered, fasted, and meditated for many years, searching for that union between the individual mind and the divine essence of the cosmos. Like all who have taken this lonely journey, he was tortured by temptations of the ego and the limitations of the physical body. But after years of discipline and concentration, he finally attained nirvana, achieving enlightenment under the now famous Bodhi Tree in Bodgaya, India. From that moment on, he maintained a state of perfect bliss, perfect wisdom, and perfect compassion—an expansion of consciousness that has been the goal of holy men for centuries. Siddhartha Gautama was then named the Buddha, or the Awakened One, as opposed to the unenlightened, those who are asleep and unaware of the true nature of time, reality, or their connection to the universe.

Upon his enlightenment, the Buddha walked to Varanasi, an important and ancient Hindu pilgrimage site. To a mere five followers in the Deer Park of Sarnath, he preached the doctrine of his newly found wisdom. He spoke of the Four Noble Truths of existence: the first, that all in this world is suffering and that disease and death are inevitable, caused by impermanence and the constantly changing nature of all things physical; the second, that this suffering is the result of ignorance and the attachment of ego to objects, other people, and the self; the third, that the way to escape reincarnation (the unending circle of suffering from life, death, and rebirth) and to achieve nirvana (the union with the deepest realization of the universe) is to eliminate the ego, the cause of desire; and the fourth, that the way to achieve this enlightenment is through the Eight-Fold Path, a doctrine of Right Action, Right Speech, and Right Thought—a structuring of behavior and consciousness to achieve harmony with the underlying forces that uphold the universe and create reality as we know it.

The Buddha retained basic Hindu concepts in his teachings: nirvana, the achievement of the highest state of consciousness; karma, the principle that every action has a consequence affecting reincarnation; and *moksha,* the liberation from karmic suffering, which can be achieved only through enlightenment.

But the Buddha went on to suffuse these tenets of Hinduism with his philosophy of equality and compassion. He began a religion free of caste and the exclusivity of the Brahmanic priesthood, making it accessible to all. He believed that enlightenment was achieved not through the physical extremes of yogic penance nor through the lavish materialism of self-indulgence, but through his path, The Middle Way.

The Buddha also expanded upon the concept of nirvana. Derived from the Sanskrit words *nir,* meaning "no," and *vana,* meaning "wind," nirvana is the state of an "empty" or "still" mind and a quiet ego, which have risen to a level of mirror-like perfection and reflect the universal spirit of Brahma. To these characteristics, the Buddha

RIGHT: A golden Buddha displays the Vitarka Mudra, a symbolic hand gesture that illustrates The Turning of the Wheel of Dharma.

OPPOSITE: With his hands forming the Dhyan Meditation Mudra, a Tibetan monk meditates in the park once called Rishi Patana, The Park of the Sages. Buddha spent several rainy seasons here with his followers and other holy men.

added the achievement of perfect wisdom and compassion: perfect wisdom resulting in a fullness of the mind, rather than just a reflection of the universal spirit; and compassion resulting in the delay of release from one's own body in order to assist in the enlightenment of others.

These revelations and reforms make up the Dharma, the underlying foundation of Buddhism. It is a religion without a god. Instead it offers a thorough analysis of the human condition, in which we as individuals are responsible for our own existence, our own spiritual evolution and ultimately our own enlightenment. At the same time, however, each of us is part of the universal consciousness that is creating reality at this very moment. The emanation of this reality and the world as we perceive it are conditioned by our sense organs, and it is only through the use of our minds that we can go beyond the limitations of our physical existence. The Buddha was "awakened" because he understood and underwent the evolution necessary to release the almost infinite potential of the mind. His supreme accomplishment has changed the way a large portion of humanity perceives reality, perhaps granting the human race the potential to unleash an unlimited future.

ABOVE: God-kings stare out from a giant
entrance gate situated at one of the
cardinal directions at Angkor Wat.

RIGHT: Four eyespots and sinuous lines
grace the dramatic, nine-inch
wingspan of a Saturnid moth camou-
flaged against the temple wall of
Prasat Kravanh

# ANGKOR

Between the eighty-seven-mile-long Tonle Sap Lake and the Kulen Hills, lay the astonishing remains of the Khmer Kingdom, one of the most majestic and artistically gifted civilizations in the world. Between A.D. 800–1200, a succession of twelve kings built royal capitals in this forbidding region; cities whose crowning glories were hundreds of temples unparalleled in the synthesis of art, architecture, and cosmology.

Settling along the the Mekong River and its tributaries, the Khmers evolved from the Fou Nan and Chen La Kingdoms. These ancient Asian cultures became indianized with the arrival of Hinduism in the first century A.D., and Buddhism shortly thereafter. The fusion of these cosmologies prompted a huge outpouring of devotional art lasting centuries, but it was not until the reign of King Jayavarman II, during which he declared himself a god by establishing the Devaraja cult, that the region was unified and a golden age began. The construction of his massive funereal monument, as well as those of subsequent kings, marked the beginning of large-scale building with an emphasis on meru-style architecture.

Other factors contributed to the exponential growth and architectural development of the Khmer kingdom. As its wealth and power increased with each succeeding king, agricultural knowledge grew more sophisticated, resulting in extraordinary engineering achievements. The Khmers devised an extensive irrigation system that harnessed the monsoon rains. They also constructed huge artificial lakes, called *barays,* that stored water during the hot, dry season, to be distributed using a complex system of dikes and canals. These marvels allowed the Khmers to produce two or three rice harvests each year and feed a population of more than one million.

The security and prosperity derived from a stable food supply allowed the Khmers to construct countless more sanctuaries and temples on an enormous architectural scale. Hundreds of elephants and thousands of oxcarts transported stone blocks from quarries twenty-five miles away, and armies of artisans carried out the intricate designs of master architects and visionary artists. The result was the magnificent city of Angkor, the "capital city," and center of the Khmer civilization. During A.D. 1100–1200, it reached its zenith and dominated Southeast Asia from the coast of Vietnam to Bagan in Myanmar, and included much of Thailand.

Today, of the over one thousand remaining temples covering an area of one hundred and twenty square miles, only about forty are accessible; the most often visited sites being Angkor Wat, Bayon and Angkor Thom, Ta Phrom, and Banteay Srei.

## ANGKOR WAT

At the end of the eleventh century, King Suryavarman II built Angkor Wat, the masterpiece of Khmer architecture. A shrine to Vishnu, it is the largest religious building in the world and took over thirty-seven years to build. As with other funereal monuments, Angkor Wat faces west into the setting sun and towards the Land of the Dead. The layout of its remarkable mathematic design forms a diagram which corresponds symbolically with the Hindu myth that describes the creation of the universe.

PAGES 110–111: In describing its incomparable perfection, the great conservator Bernard Groslier wrote that Angkor Wat was "one of the supreme architectural triumphs of all time. There can be no doubt that it was conceived by one man, by the genius of a great architect. It is a masterpiece without a successor."

PAGES 112–113: *left,* The main tower of Angkor Wat represents Meru, the center of the Hindu universe located in the Himalaya; *right,* This huge statue of Vishnu, Protector and Upholder of the Universe, has managed to remain in situ inside of Angkor Wat since its creation.

As I walked along the huge, ancient stones of the causeway leading to Angkor Wat, I was forced to look inward and question my own significance in the universe. Everything here, from the huge moat protecting the complex to the giant *nagas* flanking my path, is designed to make one shrink before the majesty of Vishnu.

After passing through a succession of courtyards, each grander and more elaborate than the last, I arrived at an enormous *meru* with its five soaring peaks and exquisitely carved walls. What a spectacle this all must have been long ago, when thousands thronged to watch as priests and attendants performed rituals and ascended the steep steps to the uppermost chambers of the gods.

Angkor Wat is the representation of the Khmer universe, reflecting a relationship to nature on such a deep level, that it makes modern architecture seem spiritually empty. The soul of the Khmer is alive in these temples and mirrored in the faces of today's Cambodians, the recipients of a rich artistic and spritual heritage.

The Gate of Victory, at the southern approach to the royal city of Angkor Thom, is lined with two long rows of colossal deities. Fifty-four stone figures stand in succession on either side—demons on the right, gods on the left. Each holds up part of a giant *naga*. This arrangement depicts the Hindu Creation Myth, found in the Bhagavata Purana and called The Churning of the Sea of Milk. In this myth, a *naga* is used to manifest the universe from the primordial, undifferentiated ocean of creation.

The decline of Angkor began with the death of Jayavarman VII. By 1431, the Royal Court had moved south, and the capital was sacked by Thailand's armies soon after. Except for a small trickle of Buddhist pilgrims visiting Angkor Wat, the area was abandoned, left to the ravages of time and the engulfing tropical forest. During a fifty-year period in the mid-sixteenth century, the glories of Angkor were briefly restored, but an unrelenting mantle of vine, moss, and root was again allowed to overtake and obscure the majestic monuments.

The outside world first learned of the opulence of Angkor's royal courts through the travel journals of a Chinese trader named Chou Ta-Kuan, who traveled along the Mekong River to Angkor Thom in 1296. But it was not until the seventeenth and eighteenth centuries, through the diaries of missionaries, that a wider European audience heard descriptions of its fantastic ruins.

By the mid-nineteenth century, the wonders of Angkor were further revealed to the cognoscenti through the surveys, photographs, and journals of adventurers who had explored its jungle. Westerners were romanced through the illustrated diaries of French naturalist and explorer Henri Mouhet, who, with the support of the Royal Geographic Society of London, visited Cambodia in 1860 to measure and survey Angkor. His exotic descriptions and beautiful color illustrations were published posthumously in 1864. In 1871, another survey of Angkor was conducted by Louis Delaporte, and in 1875, John Thomson published the first detailed photographs of the area. In 1898, L'Ecole d'Extreme Orient (The French School of the Far East) was established along with the Angkor Conservancy in Siem Reap, and from 1907 on, the French led the conservation

Built at the end of the twelfth century by Jayavarman VII, The Elephant Terrace faces the royal square of Angkor Thom, of which only the stone foundation remains. Framing the south stairway, these three-headed elephants are depicted gathering lotus flowers.

North of Angkor Wat lies the temple of Bayon—the central shrine and exact geographic center of Angkor Thom.

and restoration efforts. More than one hundred years have been spent carefully rebuilding and protecting Angkor's storehouse of religious art.

In 1974, the French conservators were forced to leave during the Cambodian civil war, a war that continues sporadically to the present. Following a cease fire signed at the Paris Peace Accord in October, 1991, Cambodian conservator Pich Keo, a one-time assistant to conservator Bernard Groslier, resumed restoration efforts.

It was feared that the war would irreparably damage Angkor, or even destroy it, but the shrines have miraculously survived; the real threat comes, as it always has, from theft, rainfall, and rapid growth of tropical vegetation. UNESCO has designated

Angkor as a World Heritage Site, and together with the World Monuments Fund, is currently coordinating its restoration. The goals are to train enough Cambodian experts in archaeology and conservation to continue the formidable task of repairing and safe-guarding what has been uncovered, and to continue the exploration of the surrounding jungle, which is believed to contain additional significant temple ruins.

Angkor's legacy is its Khmer art and architecture. Expressing the most venerable philosophies of Asia, and forming an encyclopedic storehouse of Hindu and Buddhist symbolism, they are a focus and a source of inspiration for modern Cambodia's rebirth and rediscovery.

Bayon was built one hundred years after Angkor Wat, by Jayavarman VII, the last king in the succession of Angkor god-kings.

This "cosmic mountain" was completed at
the end of the twelfth century and boasts
fifty-four towers, out of which gaze two
hundred stone faces. Facing all cardinal
directions, they represent the king in his
incarnation as the serene and compassionate
Bodhisattva Avalokitesvara.

ABOVE: The circular, central sanctuary of Bayon's
third level.

OPPOSITE: Closeup of Bodhisattva Avalokitesvara
found on Bayon's third level.

# TA PROHM

A stone path leads to the entrance of Ta Prohm.

OPPOSITE TOP AND BOTTOM:
The inner courtyards of
Ta Prohm.

One of the largest monuments in the Angkor complex is Ta Prohm, located east of Angkor Thom. Translations of inscriptions, describing the twelfth-century community, were found in situ and list an impressive population of 12,640 inhabitants—including thirteen high priests, 2,740 officials, and 615 dancers. One can only imagine how stunning the opulent Khmer courts appeared against the backdrop of verdant jungle. But like many things beautiful, this paradise of worship was tenuous and fragile; the wood and bamboo out of which it was built were ultimately no match for the forces of nature.

Gone are the shops, the palaces, the libraries, and the homes of the high priests, bureaucrats, and dancers; all have been claimed by the relentless jungle. Everything is shrouded with a suffocating mantle of vegetation. Huge beetles, millipedes, and lizards have made their homes among the ruins and every stone is covered in a rich patina of algae, moss, and lichen. Today, Ta Prohm remains unrestored, but a mysterious haunting beauty has taken hold—as permeating as the massive roots of the giant fig and silk cotton trees that now claim ownership over it—making it one of the most evocative sites at Angkor.

ABOVE AND OPPOSITE: Miniature in scale compared to
Angkor Wat, Banteay Srei is exquisitely carved from
pink laterite to mimic the wooden temples of its era.
Built in A.D. 967, this Citadel of Women is completely
covered with maidens, classically proportioned Khmer
gods, and scenes from the Ramayana Epic, all of which
are intertwined with flowers and foliage.

RIGHT: Yama, God of the Underworld.

LEFT: *Nagas* decorate the cornerstone of a doorway at Banteay Srei.

PAGES 124–125: Sunrise at Srah Srang, a royal bathing pool nearly one-half-mile long and almost one thousand feet wide.

123

*Apsaras,* meaning "waters of essence," are the nymph goddesses born from the foam of the milky ocean and represent the ideal of Khmer beauty. In Angkor Wat alone, seventeen hundred of these courtesans appear on temple walls. Surrounded by flower motifs, they wear elaborate jewels, crowns, and hair ornaments.

# JAVA

Giant pads (*above*) and water lilies (*below*) thrive in an ornamental pond at the Bogor Botanical Garden.

On a stream on the Prambanan Plain, young boys ride home-made boats constructed from banana trees.

# BOROBUDUR

On the verdant Kedu Plain on the garden island of Java, lies Borobudur, the largest Buddhist monument in the world. Built upon a sacred confluence between the Elo and Progo Rivers—representing India's holy Ganges and Yamuna Rivers—this "cosmic mountain" is a marvel of stone and a monolithic symbol of Buddhist enlightenment. Begun by King Samaratungga more than eleven hundred years ago, Borobudur took generations to complete.

Constructed from almost two million blocks of volcanic stone, Borobudur conforms to the basic shape, design, and architectural symbolism of an enormous Buddhist stupa. The structure's exterior is covered with painstakingly designed details; more than four hundred Buddhas sit in perfect serenity, each in its own meditation cave adorning the outside of the temple.

If seen from above, Borobudur appears as a huge mandala, a sacred diagram in the shape of the cosmic lotus. Incorporated into the actual layout of the monument, this mandala guides pilgrims on their symbolic journey to nirvana.

Pilgrims enter Borobudur from any one of its four directional portals. Once inside, they begin their journey to the top of the stupa by circumambulating—walking clockwise—through its ten gradually ascending levels, passing galleries that display nearly fifteen hundred pictorial reliefs. Hundreds of stone panels surround the galleries and depict comprehensive narratives from Buddhist history, such as the Lalitaristra, the Life

One of the 1,460 carved panels of Borobudur shows a trading vessel of the type which carried over the Indian colonists who later established Buddhism in Java.

The southern foot of Borobudur.

This uncovered, latticed stupa is one of seventy-two found on the uppermost terraces of Borobudur.

OPPOSITE TOP: Each of these latticed stupas covers a Buddha effigy.

OPPOSITE BOTTOM: Four hundred thirty-two Buddhas are niched into Borobudur's exterior walls. Each sits in its own meditation cave and displays one of six *mudras*.

of Buddha; the Jataka, a collection of ornately illustrated poems; and the Karmawibhangga, a description of the doctrine of karma.

The final circle of the journey leads pilgrims to Borobudur's top level, its mystical focal point. Against the backdrop of brooding volcanos is a circle of seventy-two trellised stupas, each of which contains a carved Buddha gesturing one of six mudras.

Rising above this circle of meditating Buddhas is Borobudur's second, uppermost *garbha*. Topped by a stone spire, this "womb" at one time concealed a golden Buddha in a secret chamber. The significance of this *garbha* is that it represents the Buddha Nature, or Tathagata Garbha (*tathagata* = suchness; *garbha* = womb). It is the state of potential from which all reality is manifested. Buddha, as The Enlightened One, is one and the same with this state of "suchness."

# PRAMBANAN

The largest Hindu shrine in Indonesia is Candi Laradjonggrang, built in the ninth century on the Prambanan Plain near Yogyakarta, Java. It is the tallest and most elegant of the approximately fifty remaining Hindu and Buddhist temples of the Sanjaya Dynasty and its Javanese kingdom that thrived during A.D. 800–1000. Its main temples and more than four hundred smaller shrines are scattered throughout several square miles and constitute the greatest concentration of sacred architecture in Indonesia.

Erected from immense blocks of stone, these eastern-facing temples overlook the holy Opek River and stand within sight of Mount Merapi, an active volcano worshiped by the early Javanese. Built in the image of a Maha Meru, or the Great Mountains of the Gods, they were designed as shrines to the Hindu Trimurti of Brahma, Vishnu, and

One of eighty-six finely carved balustrade panels of the
Shiva temple at Prambanan depicts Shiva as Dewa
Lokapala, God of the Winds.

RIGHT: A silhouette of Candi Laradjonggrang's three towers
built on the Prambanan Plain and dedicated to the
Trimurti: Brahma, Vishnu, and Shiva.

Shiva. Their levels of construction represent the three spheres of the cosmos: the base as the underworld; the body as the middle world; and the spire as the upper world. Surrounding each temple group are three concentric courtyards, each one more sacred than the one preceding it.

    The main temple of the group is Candi Shiva. Its slender spires, resembling craggy Himalayan pinnacles, soar more than one hundred fifty feet into the sky and are covered with celestial beings and detailed ornamentation. Hundreds of stone panels

Ganesh, Elephant Son of Shiva and Remover of Obstacles, sits in the western inner sanctum of Candi Shiva in Prambanan.

OPPOSITE: Candi Laradjonggrang is believed to be the reliquary of King Batitung. Ashes and various symbols of the cosmos were found in a casket deep within a well shaft of the candi. Celebrated for its detailed panels of the Hindu Ramayana, the temple is topped by stupa-shaped *ratnas,* architectural evidence of the peaceful coexistence of Buddhist and Hindu beliefs.

Manicured gardens surround Candi Kalasan, a Buddhist temple built by King Panangkaranin in A.D. 778 to honor Tara, Goddess of Compassion.

Candi Menduit, which dates from A.D. 800, was a purification and preparation temple for pilgrims heading to Borobudur. It contains three of the finest pieces of sculpture in Java. Its centerpiece is a Sakyamuni Buddha seated on his Prabha throne with his hands in the Pravartana Mudra position that signifies the teaching of religion.

depicting the Ramayana fill the mid-level galleries, while images of serene ascetics meditating among stupa-like *ratnas,* cover the exterior.

Like the Angkor temples of Cambodia, the Prambanan temples also served as funereal monuments for kings whose ashes were buried in wells located deep below the foundations. An image of the corresponding Hindu god of which the king was an incarnation topped the well, and temple spires crowned the celestial mausoleum.

Unlike most Javanese temples, which incorporate strictly Hindu or Buddhist iconography, Candi Shiva and other shrines of Laradjonggrang feature a unique and ingenious combination of Hindu and Buddhist symbolism. Utilizing both stupa and *lingam* imagery, Prambanan presents a synthesis of prehistoric ancestor and Shiva worship.

The ruins of the main gate of Kraton Ratu Boko, the
ninth-century palace of King Boko.

Troupes of men representing their individual villages arrive from all parts of Java to Candi Prambanan to participate in the annual horse dance competition called the Gatilan. Dressed in traditional folk costumes and accompanied by a gamelan orchestra, they compete in mock battles riding upon their rattan horses.

OPPOSITE: Anggora Prasetya and Prastiwi, two members from the Royal Classical Yogyanese Dance Company from the Sultan's Palace, reenact scenes from the Ramayana in front of the imposing entrances of Candi Sari and Candi Sewu.

# THAILAND

A country which has never seen colonial rule, Thailand traces its political roots back to the seventh-century Namchao Kingdom of Yunnan, China. Though Buddhism had been introduced as early as A.D. 200 to the peoples inhabiting the area, it was not until the thirteenth century that the religion was institutionalized, bringing about the unification of the Thai empire and its culture.

Bangkok's significant role in Thailand began in 1782, when the first of the Chakri Dynasty kings, Rama I (Chao Phaya Chakri) established it as the capital. He built it in the image of Ayutthaya—an ancient royal city sacked by the Burmese in 1767—and it soon became the economic and religious heart of Thailand.

Monk Tani Sudasna sits in front of the Buddha inside Wat Saket in Bangkok, Thailand.

OPPOSITE TOP: Built in 1899, Wat Benjamabopit, The Marble Temple, was the last significant royal temple to be built in Bangkok. It is unique in its use of white Carrara marble, Western-style stained glass, and yellow Chinese tiles.

OPPOSITE BOTTOM: To reach Golden Mount, one must climb a 318-step stairway leading to the top of a man-made hill, the highest elevation in Bangkok at over 250 feet. The gilded *chedi,* or stupa, contains valuable Buddha relics.

ABOVE: Built in the late 1800s, Loha
Prasay, The Iron Palace, is modeled
after a Sri Lankan palace and represents a legendary Buddhist pavilion.

RIGHT: Ethnic Chinese make up a large
percentage of Thailand's population.
At this Joss temple, they light
incense, perform ancestor worship,
and divine the future by shaking
numbered joss sticks in a canister,
randomly selecting a stick, and
matching its number with fortunes
found in an ancient, temple cabinet.

ABOVE: Young monk initiates take their exams under the watchful eyes of Buddha in Wat Suthat, one of the most important temples in Bangkok.

LEFT: Devotees at Wat Rajabopit await a holy water blessing. This temple was built in 1863 by King Chulalongkorn, whose personal taste created a unique Thai temple that blends Western and Thai architectural styles, and bears a striking resemblance to an Italian Gothic cathedral.

Though ninety-four percent of the population is Buddhist, the propitiation of animistic *phi* spirits still forms the foundation of Thai beliefs. *Phar phums,* or spirit houses, are found throughout the entire country, blending in with modern architecture and high technology. These miniature temples are found in homes, workplaces, and public areas. In addition to the *phar phums,* over twenty-seven thousand temples, or *wats,* occupy a place of paramount importance in Thai society. Their unique architectural style and superb use of gold, carved wood, bronze, and ceramic and colored glass tiles impart a shimmering, magical quality to Thai shrines.

LEFT: Built in 1382 and containing Buddhist relics, the gilded and copper-plated Wat Prathat Doi Suthep sits atop the the forested Doi Pui Hill, overlooking the city of Chiang Mai.

BELOW: Pra Seewali, a young monk from Sri Lanka, takes time away from his rigorous study and meditation to discuss philosophy and world politics at Nakon Pathom *chedi.*

The famous Emerald Buddha, carved from a single piece of jade, is the most revered image in Thailand. The first historic record of its origin is 1434, when lightening struck the *chedi* at Chiang Rai and cracked open the Buddha's plaster covering, exposing the jade Buddha underneath. It became the talisman of the king's sovereignty and, after a thirty-year stay at Lampang, was moved to the Lanna Kingdom's capital city of Chiang Mai. A subsequent king who was half-Laotian took it with him to Laos where it remained for two hundred years. It was eventually recovered by the Thais and installed in their Thonburi capital. The Buddha's journey ended in 1778 at the royal chapel, Phra Kaeo, in King Rama's I newly built capital city of Bangkok. Enshrined upon an eleven-foot altar, it has three jackets of gold and diamonds that are changed seasonally by the king.

LEFT: Phra Sri Ratana, erected by King Rama IV, stands on the Upper Terrace in the Grand Palace temple compound in Bangkok. Phra Mondop, the palace's library, is seen here in the middle; the Royal Pantheon is on the right.

Streams of Thai pilgrims and tourists visit the
Grand Palace, Thailand's most popular shrine.

In Thai culture, Buddhism and the monarchy are inseparable.
Since the time of King Rama III, it has been the custom for all kings to
become ordained monks at Wat Bournivet prior to ascending the
throne; King Rama IV (Mongkut) served there for twenty-seven years
before his rule. Religious education is equally important for the com-
mon people. Traditionally, every Thai male becomes a monk for at least
three months; some go on to train for a lifetime. It is estimated that
there are more than two hundred-fifty thousand monks in Thailand
practicing the Theravedin form of Buddhism.

Though modern Thailand is the economic powerhouse of
Southeast Asia, there is a seamless connection between its industrializa-
tion and its spirituality. Regardless of technological advancement and
monetary success, what will always remain strong in Thailand is the rich
heritage of religion, art, and architecture based on the belief in the great
truths of Buddhism and the mystical powers of animistic spirits.

The Mahamotien, built in the late 1700s, con-
sists of three chambers: the Amarindra Vinichai
Hall for ceremonies of the Court; the Paisal
Coronation Hall; and the original residence of
the first three Rama kings of the Chakri
Dynasty. Atop the tiled roofs are ornamental
*chofa*— a Thai term for "sky tassels"—representing the elongated neck of Garuda.

ABOVE: A pipal, or "wisdom tree," in the courtyard of
   Wat Pho is honored by a saffron-colored wrap.

OPPOSITE TOP: Wat Pho (Phra Chetuphon), situated
   adjacent to the Grand Palace, is the oldest
   monastery in Bangkok, as evidenced by this pre-
   Buddhist *lingam.*

OPPOSITE BOTTOM: Decorated with gold leaf and flowers, a venerable stone *lingam* marks the entrance of
   Wat Phra Kaeo.

PAGES 154–155: Made of brick, covered with
   plaster, and finished with gold leaf, this
   massive Buddha at Wat Pho is the largest
   reclining Buddha in Thailand. It mea-
   sures 145 feet long and 50 feet high and
   depicts Buddha as he passed from this
   world into his final nirvana.

The Royal Pantheon is topped by a towering Khmer-style *prang*, covered in multicolored, mirrored-glass tiles, and surmounted by a Hindu thunderbolt, the symbol of Shiva.

OPPOSITE AND PAGE 158: Mosaics and ceramic flowers embellish two of Wat Po's four *chedi*s, built as memorials to the Chakri kings, the first rulers of Bangkok.

ABOVE: The Phra Sri Ratana *chedi* at Wat
Phra Kaeo.

PAGE 160: *top left and right,* Latt and Nung
of the Sukhothai Culture Center
Dance Troupe dance in the same place
as their ancestors before them, at the
ruins of Sukhothai; *bottom,* Phiriaporn
Sujaree of the Old Chiang Mai Culture
Center Dance Troupe, stands before
the giant *naga* staircase of Wat Chedi
Luang. She displays the long nails
worn for a northern Thai dance performed to greet honored guests.

PAGE 161: Latt, Ghung, and Nung dance
joyously before Wat Mahathat in
Sukhothai.

The fourteenth-century Wat Si Chum at Sukhothai is filled completely by the enormous seated image of Phra Ashana Buddha.

The Buddha's hand is so large that a man standing before it would only measure up to its thumb. It is in the Bhusparsha Mudra, or "earth touching" position, signifying the earth bearing witness to Buddha's enlightenment.

PAGE 164: *top left,* Wat Phumin, Nan; *top right,* Wat Lampang Luang, Lampang; *middle left,* Wat Phrasingh, Chiang Mai; *middle right,* Prasat Phra Debidorn in front of Royal Pantheon, Bangkok; *bottom left,* Wat Phrasingh, Chiang Mai; *bottom right,* Wat Umong, Chiang Mai.

PAGE 165: A Buddha from Ayutthaya. It is said there are more Buddha images than people in Thailand. From miniature amulets worn around the neck, to huge, golden temple statues, the sheer number is an undeniable testament to Thailand's thirteen hundred years of devotion to Buddha's spiritual ideas.

# MYANMAR

## SHWEDAGON

OPPOSITE: An elegant landscape of golden spires and mythical guardians surrounds the shrine of Shwedagon. Pilgrims often arrive before dawn to light votive candles and pray.

PAGES 168–169: The Pyatthat Pavilion provides a place of respite for pilgrims.

The venerable history of Shwedagon stretches back over twenty-five hundred years to the legend of Taphussa and Bhallika, two merchants on a trading mission to India. Guided by a *nat* spirit—one of many animistic deities—they were led to a bodhi tree under which sat Buddha, newly enlightened and in prayerful meditation. Taphussa and Bhallika offered the Buddha their honey cakes, and in gratitude, he bestowed upon them eight of his sacred hairs.

The men brought this holy treasure back to Yangon to be enshrined in an ancient cave temple atop Singuttara Hill. As they excavated down into the center of the hill to reach the shrine, they came upon the relics of three previous Buddhas—a staff, a water dipper, and a robe—items once belonging to mendicants, holy men destined for enlightenment who walked the land thousands of years ago. These relics, together with the Buddha's hairs, were placed in a jeweled chest said to have been made by Sakka, King of the Nats. The chest was placed in the shrine and the opening to the cave temple was sealed by a heavy slab of gold upon which was built a small, golden pagoda.

Throughout the centuries and the unbroken reigns of thirty-two kings, this cherished and holy site was worshiped and lovingly maintained. Marking the passage of time, successive pagodas were built, each on top of the last, using bricks of silver, tin, copper, lead, and marble. A final iron-brick pagoda was built to cover the whole, forming the core of what is today the richest pagoda in the world: a massive shrine rising 326 feet, covered with sixty tons of gold, and encrusted with more than fifteen thousand diamonds and other precious stones.

A treasury of Buddhist art and Burmese history, Shwedagon is visible from virtually any point in Yangon, but its spiritual presence extends much further, sweeping over the entire country of Myanmar. Shwedagon is not only a sanctuary for prayer and meditation, but also a lively meeting place, a daily stop for citizens who wish to pay respect to the beliefs that guide their lives.

There is a timeless sanctity that infuses and protects Shwedagon, a steady, undiminished force, that even in modern times continues to draw hundreds of thousands of pilgrims each year from Buddhist communities as far away as Korea, Japan, and remote regions of China. It is a spiritual focal point for the people of Southeast Asia and the golden symbol of Buddha's transcendent enlightenment.

Encountering Shwedagon is an experience
that is as beautiful as it is meaningful.
Arriving before dawn, we approach the
great shrine in darkness. Following dim
silhouettes, we travel up a long, dark stairway that brings us out onto the cold, wet
marble terrace and into the caress of incense
mingled with the sweet scents of jasmine
and magnolia. The sounds of more than a
thousand gold and silver bells surrounding
its spire drift through the air and mix in
gentle harmony with hushed and reverential
whispers. Our eyes are drawn upward,
where a faint glimmer drifts within the fog—
and suddenly, like mountains appearing
through a breaking storm—the huge dome
of Shwedagon appears. The brilliance of its
bell-shaped spire shimmers through the
gauzy mist as if a mirage, apt to disappear at
any moment. Terraces of extravagant spires
and more than one hundred additional
shrines encircle the radiant stupa For the
briefest of moments, they capture the delicate tint of dawn and bear an otherworldly
resemblance to the ice-clad peaks of the
Himalaya.

     As we slowly circle the base in a
respectful clockwise direction, an oracle cave
and planetary prayer posts with their
ancient inscriptions guide us. Surrounded
by the powers of prayer and devotion of
those nearby, a spiritual energy envelopes us.
We continue moving, awed by Shwedagon's
beauty and amazed that this magic can still
be experienced on the eve of the twenty-first
century. We stop at an uncommonly large
tree that has grown within sight of the golden
dome for centuries. It a sacred bodhi tree
taken as a sapling from the original banyon
under which Buddha attained his enlightenment. How fitting that monks continue to
sit beneath this symbol of Buddha and to
search for the peace and rapture of his wisdom.

The power and resonance of the
stupa shape continually repeats
throughout the grounds of
Shwedagon. Clusters of stupas
in various sizes concentrate the
prayers of the devotee.

With such a surrounding, the
mind cannot long resist being
channeled into focused prayer
and meditation.

Fine wood carvings and mosaics decorate the exterior
of the Konagamana Adoration Hall, while giant bells
and Buddha images are housed inside.

Shwedagon's base is surrounded by three groups of
pagodas: sixty-four small pagodas circle the entire
stupa; four larger-size pagodas mark off the corners of
its base; and the four largest occupy the midpoint of
each side.

OPPOSITE: A monk meditates in front of the 326-foot Shwedagon.

LEFT: Whether for meditations, petitions, or prayers, many pilgrims who come to Shwedagon stay for several days. Among the worshipers seen here are nuns dressed in their traditional pink robes.

BELOW: The discipline of meditation, chanting, and the study of sacred text prepares the mind to accept and understand Buddha's Middle Way.

OVERLEAF: One hundred twenty-eight steps lead to the northern entrance to Shwedagon.

# BAGAN

Sunrise on the Bagan Plain.

Spread along eight miles of the Ayeryawaddy River in Myanmar, lie the ruins of a once vast and royal city and one of the most wondrous landscapes in the world, Bagan. Covering more than sixteen square miles of desolate plateau, it was once one of Asia's most advanced cultures and the most elegant holy city ever constructed.

According to the Glass Palace Chronicle of the Kings of Burma, the official recorded history of the country, Bagan was founded in A.D. 108 by King Thamudarit, the first in an unbroken dynasty of fifty-five kings. However, it was not until the reign of its forty-second king, Anawrahta, in A.D. 1044, that Bagan began to effect a strong influence on the country's political and spiritual unification.

178

In A.D. 1075, King Anawrahta conquered the Mons, a pre-Buddhist people, and transferred their sacred relics and holy Pali Theravedic Scriptures from the their capital of Thaton to Bagan. The arrival of these religious treasures on the backs of thirty-two royal, white elephants, and their subsequent installation in the city, affirmed the supreme holiness of Bagan and its new role as the center of Burmese society. With power established, King Anawrahta employed the talents and labor of thousands of artisans, craftsmen, and Buddhist monks, setting into motion an explosion of architectural and artistic creation that continued for the next two centuries.

By the reign of Bagan's final king, Naranthihapate, Bagan boasted an astonishing

Sunset on the Ayeryawaddy River.

It was during the reign of King Narathu that construction of Dhammayangyi began, but fate would not allow the king to see it to completion. He had assumed the throne by killing both his father and brother in their sleep, and during his reign, ordered the execution of one of his queens. In an act of revenge, the queen's father sent an assassin, dressed as a Brahman priest, to kill Narathu.

One of the five thousand surviving shrines on the Bagan Plain.

OPPOSITE: Sulamani dates from A.D. 1183 and was built by King Narapathisithu, son of assassinated King Narathu.

collection of thirteen thousand religious buildings, including libraries, monasteries, temples, and stupas. They incorporated a bewildering variety of architectural styles, including stone replicas of Indian cave temples, Sinhalese stupas, and shrines dedicated to Meru, the mountain home of Shiva. Many were intricately embellished with stucco carvings, glazed sandstone friezes, and summits crowned with elegant spires.

As a cultural and religious capital, Bagan was a seat of advanced Buddhist thought and religious teaching, and home to a great Pali university where the ancient scriptures were studied. This age of growth and enlightenment lasted until the invasion of Kublai Kahn in 1287, when the first of the city's temples were disassembled to build defense walls. The passage of time saw additional architecture fall victim to invaders, vandals, and at least ten earthquakes leaving Bagan in its present, poetically derelict condition. Although the outlines, foundations, and ruins of more than five thousand original temples still exist, only about one hundred have been restored to their original splendor.

The introduction of Buddhist thought and religion to the Burmese people was eased by the preservation of pre-Buddhist animistic *nat* worship. Incorporated into Buddhism and allowed to occupy shrines in this courtyard at Shwezigon, these familiar thirty-seven *nat* deities helped the Burmese people assimilate the new national religion.

OPPOSITE: Shwezigon is one of the earliest models of a Burmese stupa, or pagoda. Its construction was begun by King Anawrahta and finished by his son King Kyanzittha at the end of the eleventh century.

Each morning, monks leave their chambers to beg for rice, their one and only meal of the day. Those who provide them with this sustenance are considered to have gained merit.

Nevertheless, Bagan remains an important pilgrimage site for the people of Myanmar and vestiges of its golden era can still be found at points along the Ayeryawaddy River: Shwezigon, built by King Kyanzittha in A.D. 1048, houses the sacred tooth and frontal bone of the Buddha; Ananda—its white and gold *sikhara* inspired by a mythological meditation cave—enshrines four colossal standing Buddhas and a unique collection of glazed tiles depicting the Buddhist Jataka stories. These spectacular shrines and thousands of other holy reliquaries are regarded as extraordinary places of worship. They are testaments to the deep reverence and honor for Gautama Buddha by a people whose spiritual commitment created a city imbued with his essence.

OPPOSITE: Lemyethna was built in 1222 by Minister Anantathura.

Built in A.D. 1091 by King Kyanzittha, Ananda is one of the four largest pagodas in Myanmar. Its white-washed appearance and cruciform design are meant to honor the cave temples found in the snow-covered Nandamula Mountains of the Himalaya.

189

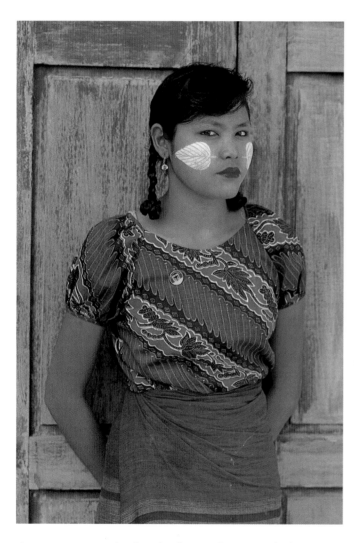

A young woman displays bodhi tree leaves applied
to her cheeks with *thanaka,* a cosmetic made of
jasmine and sandlewood paste.

A goat farmer tends his flock on the
Bagan Plain near the Ayeryawaddy
River.

A girl, traditionally dressed in a *longyi,* or sarong, rests against a temple column at Bagan.

LEFT: A young monk sits by a guardian lion in the white-washed courtyard of Ananda in Bagan.

191

# LADAKH

The mighty Indus River snakes its way through the eroded gorges of the arid Ladakh Range of the Himalaya.

Along the western edge of the Tibetan Plateau lies a windswept desert land, a high altitude moonscape hidden along the outermost ranges of the Himalaya. Called Ladakh, or Land of the Passes, it is bisected by the great Indus River and encompasses forty-five thousand square miles of high peaks, glaciers, and steep rocky gorges.

Ladakh was an autonomous kingdom for more than a thousand years, part of an extensive Vajrayana Buddhist empire whose political and religious influence once included Tibet, Sikkim, Bhutan, and the trans-Himalayan regions of Nepal. Since the reign of its first king, Mya Tri Tsangpo, in the third century B.C., Ladakh had been the meeting point for several Asian trading routes, including the famous Silk Road. Great caravans of camels, yaks, donkeys, and horses from Tibet, Kashmir, China, Afghanistan, and Turkestan converged in Leh, the kingdom's capital, to trade silk, salt, tea, grain, precious stones, and gold.

Unfortunately, Ladakh's remote location between China, India, and Pakistan made it strategically important and vulnerable to outside invasion. It was divided between India and Pakistan in 1947 and became a district of the Indian state of Jammu-

Kashmir. The caravans were discontinued in 1951, when the Red Chinese closed the border passes of Tibet, and political conflicts with India closed the Ladakh border with Pakistan. Protected by an impenetrable barrier of serrated peaks, Ladakh's monasteries and lamistic theocracy were spared from the Chinese Communist purges of Tibet during the 1950s, but it was again divided between India and China during a 1962 border war. Despite its fragmentation, Ladakh remains an immense, sparsely inhabited domain of self-sufficient hamlets and ancient monasteries.

A cultural and geographical crossroads, Ladakh is diversely populated by Baltis, a Shia Muslim tribe from central Asia; Dards, animists with distinctly Caucasian features; and Ladakhis, Buddhists of Tibetan stock. These inhabitants must cope with severe topographic and climatic extremes. Situated almost entirely above nine thousand feet, Ladakh averages only three inches of precipitation a year, and is so cold that the growing season lasts only three months a year. The Ladakhi people have learned to conserve and utilize the precious resources of their stark and barren world, using every drop of glacial melt for irrigation, every green weed for fodder, and every piece of dung for fertilizer.

The monasteries of Ladakh were hidden among remote mountains and fortified by local kings to protect them from numerous invaders, such as the Tibetans in 1530, the Mongols in 1685, and the Indian Maharajah of Jammu in 1834. King Senge Namgyal constructed the monastic village of Chemre as a home for the Kagyupa Buddhist Sect.

Ladakh was considered a Tibetan province for much of its history, and held the city of Leh as its western capital. Lechen Palkhar, the towering nine-story royal palace built by King Senge Namgyal in 1620, is second only to the Potala Palace of Lhasa as the largest example of Tibetan-style architecture.

They have survived in a place where plants and animals cling to the edge of existence.

This forbidding environment allowed Ladakh to achieve an unusual ecological and spiritual balance that gave rise to the Tibetan monastic culture. Walled monastic cities were built, utilizing the treacherous topography. They took advantage of remote valleys and impossibly sheer cliffs for protection. These *gompas,* or lamasaries, became the religious and artistic storehouses of Ladakhi culture and provided a refuge where the magnificent heritage of Tibetan ritual, prayer, and art could continue.

Early Ladakhi people practiced a religion called Bon Po, an animistic worship presided over by Shamanistic priests. These lamas officiated over rituals propitiating a pantheon filled with demons and deities who inhabited the peaks, caves, and passes, controlling all aspects of daily life, especially health and safe passage through the Himalaya.

In the seventh century, Mahayana Buddhism, was introduced to Ladakh and

then to Tibet by the great guru, Padmasambhava. This sect of Buddhism absorbed Bon Po and evolved into Vajrayana Buddhism, or the "thunderbolt vehicle." The name Vajrayana refers to the *vajra,* or *dorje*—a scepter and symbolic tool used to control the electrical, illuminating power of Buddhist enlightenment. This animistic, shamanistic Buddhism still survives in Ladakh and is divided into two branches: the old sect of the Red Hats, or the Ningmapa; and the reformed sect of the Yellow Hats, or the Gelugpa.

Today, Ladakh balances delicately between its traditional existence and the encroachment of the modern world. It is exposed to a steady stream of tourists who come to witness a timeless way of life through monastic rituals and festivals. Despite this modern "cultural invasion," the Ladakhis hold fast to the mystical poetry of their Tibetan Buddhist rituals by appeasing the spirits and demons they believe will inhabit the mountains and rivers forever.

Prayer flags strung from the ruins of a fifth-century Dard castle overlooking Leh catch the winds sweeping down from the Tibetan Plateau and send prayers to the gods.

PAGES 196–197: Dating from the 1400s, Tiktse Monestary is a thriving community of eighty Gelugpa monks. Horns, gongs, drums, and continual chants echo from the hilltop at dawn.

These gentle monks from the monastery at Likir live a solemn and mostly silent existence, eating only *tsampa,* a mixture of roasted barley and rice. It is hard to believe that their watchdog, a huge Tibetan mastiff, thrives on the same fare.

RIGHT: Young students studying outside of the Hemis Monastery. It is the custom among the Bhotia people from Tibet for the second eldest son to become a monk. Monastic schools benefit even those who do not take lifetime vows by teaching reading, writing, and mathematics, in addition to knowledge of sacred texts.

OPPOSITE: The compassionate eyes of Maitreya, Buddha of the Future, gaze serenely from the Tikste Monastery.

Ladakhis love to don their traditional finery for dancing at festivals. Tsewang Dolma wears a typical top hat called a *tibi* or *sahru*. Fashionable for both sexes, it is worn slightly cocked to one side. Her family's fortune in precious jewelry graces her neck and a goat skin wrap protects her clothing while she carries her basket.

Phunchok Angchou wears a maroon, ankle-length, woolen robe tied at the waist called a *coss*. His hat is made from pashima goat hair which is renowned for its fine, silky texture.

Monks and nuns rest along a steep trail leading to
RiDzong, The Mountain Fortress. The monastery is
perched at 11,500 feet at the back of a narrow valley overlooking apricot groves and a stream. The nuns reside at a
lower elevation in a small community called Julichen, trans-
lated as "supplied with apricots."

The nuns have a reciprocal relationship with the
monks. They tend to the apricots trees, crush apricot pits
for lamp oil, and spin wool in return for protection, food,
and holy texts. Although their strict order prohibits personal
possessions, one nun happily accepted a gift of a photo-
graph of the Dalai Lama—the exiled Tibetan leader who is
worshiped as an incarnation of the Buddha.

On the roof of the Tiktse Monastery, monks start the day by blowing ceremonial horns heard for miles across the wide Indus River Valley. The haunting sound focuses the mind and calls the faithful to prayer. In the distance, the rugged snow-capped peaks of the Ladakh Range form the Tibetan border.

PAGES 204–205: Frescoes from walls of meditation chapels at the Likir and Lamayuru Monasteries vividly portray the terrifying deities of the Vajrayana Buddhist pantheon. During meditation, Tantric Buddhists summon these demonic forces, representing the desires and temptations of the ego, in order to gain control over them.

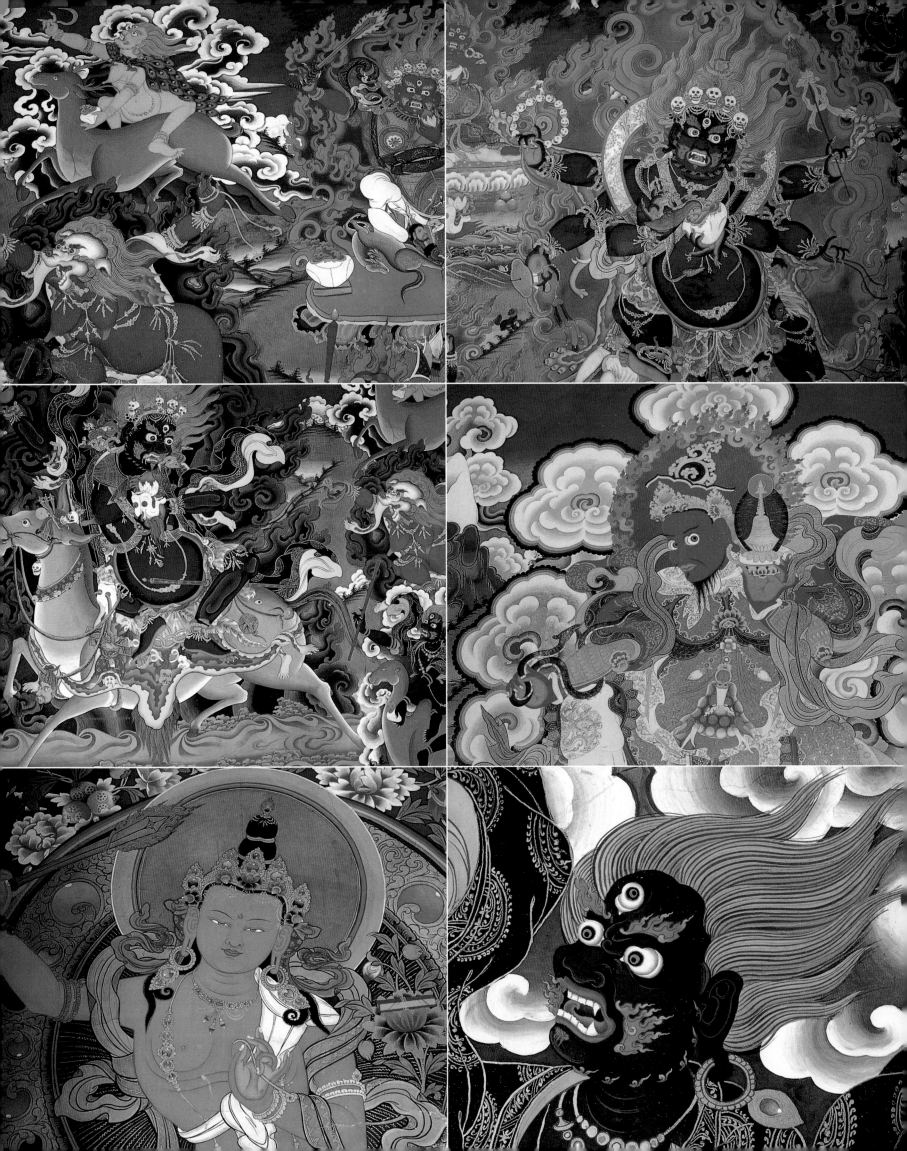

# BALI

Of all the locations in the world, the island of Bali best exemplifies the concept of sacred topography. Religion is the dominant force in the Balinese culture. On this Island of the Gods, every aspect of life is centered around ritual and prayer and involves the landscape or the calendar. Geographic space is divided into the sacred and profane, and time is considered auspicious or inauspicious.

There are an estimated twenty thousand temples in Bali exalting the thousands of deities inhabiting every mountain, river, forest, and home. A temple is considered to be any place where a deity is honored with offerings and ritual worship called *yadna*. Whether one is performing a ritual in an elaborate temple or kneeling before a vermilion-daubed rock at the edge of a jungle stream, equal respect and devotion is paid to both the greatest celestial deities and the smallest animistic spirits. And for almost every shrine an odelon, or anniversary celebration, is held also making Bali the Island of Festivals.

The all-encompassing religious devotion of the Balinese can be traced back to the unique evolution of their form of Hinduism. Beginning around the seventh century, the island was influenced by a series of religious doctrines which included Indian Shivism, Mahayana Buddhism, Tantric Buddhism, and a Javanese form of Hinduism from the Majapahit Empire. These complex philosophies combined with existing animism and ancestor worship to develop into the spectacularly ornate form of Balinese Hinduism seen today—an amalgam of Buddhist and Hindu doctrines based on the Shiva and Vishnu sects.

Like the people of India, the Balinese believe in the Hindu Creation Myth, where Brahma, known to them as Sanghyang Widhi, creates the Trisakti—the trinity of Hindu gods who, for eternity, alternately emanate and destroy the universe. This trinity is worshiped in almost every temple and is represented through the three symbolic, stone-carved seats for the gods, known as the Padmasana, or Lotus Throne.

For the Balinese, the universe exists on three levels: the upper world of gods that is light; the lower world of demons that is dark; and the middle world of humans that is both light and dark. Every aspect of human life is governed by this opposition manifested as good and evil, or the sacred and defiled. This interplay also represents the powers of the universe—Shiva and Shakti, or male and female. These forces can only be balanced through Dewa Yadnya, the ceremonies which honor the gods. As in Indian ceremonies, they involve ritual worship (*puja*), devotional prayer (*bakti*), and purification rites that propitiate the deities, demons, and the protective spirits.

The pristine blossom of a lotus, the symbol of purity, rises from the mud of the ancient pond at Pura Saraswati in Ubud, Bali.

The holiest sanctuary in Bali is Pura Besakih, The Mother Temple—a complex of twenty-two temples built upon seven terraces on the slopes of Bali's highest volcano, Gunung Agung. Ceremonies and sacrifices at Besakih pre-date Hinduism and are continued today by throngs of worshippers who present offerings and receive holy water. In 1963, as preparations for the Eka Dasa Rudra purification rites began, Gunung Agung erupted killing thousands and spewing lava to within a few feet of the temple.

The Balinese believe that their island is a paradise that can only be occupied with the permission of the spirits that reside in its landscape. Conforming to classic Hindu symbolism, all volcanoes in Bali represent the Himalaya and are inhabited by the gods. The rivers flowing down from them, such as the Ayung or Pakerisan, represent the purification and sustenance of the Ganges. The concept of holy water is so important, that the Balinese named their religion, Agama Tirtha, or "religion of the holy water." Almost every spring, pond, and *prayag* is protected and sanctified as the embodiment of divine nectar, or *amrita*. Rice grown from this water is the sacred gift, or *prasad*, of Dewi Sri, the Goddess of the Harvest. All Balinese rituals begin with *banten,* or offerings: first of fire (incense); then of water, purifying the temple and congregation; and finally of prayer. Priests known as *pedandas* then recite prayers of invitation, requesting the deities to descend to earth and occupy the temple. Offers of flowers and fruit for the gods are placed high up on bamboo towers, while offerings for the demons are laid on the ground. Holy water from venerated springs and rivers is sprinkled on the heads of worshippers, the remainder of which is divided among family members for daily use.

Temples and shrines throughout Bali are attributed with numerous levels of

sanctity. At the highest and most venerated level is Besakih, the Mother Temple, perched atop the slopes of the island's largest and most dangerous volcano, Gunung Agung. Once a pre-Hindu sacrificial site, Besakih has evolved over centuries into a huge complex of more than twenty-two temples and hundreds of smaller shrines. It is part of the Sad-Kahyangan, or the Six Great Sanctuaries—homes of the gods and seats of great wisdom and power. Second in order of sanctity are the Nine Directional Temples that radiate from Besakih like the eight petals of a lotus, covering the island with a protective mandala.

Individual temples make up the third level of sanctity. Some are associated with the island's geography: Pura Bukits, the mountain temples and Pura Segara, the sea temples. Other temples are associated with human affairs: Pura Dalem, the temples of the dead; Pura Subak, the temples of rice cultivation; and Pura Dewata, the temples of the protective deities.

Many additional levels of sanctity apply to the remaining shrines that are home to protective spirits found throughout villages, streets, and homes; even trees have their own resident deities called *tonyas*.

The 7,064-foot peak of Gunung Abang rises above Batur Crater and the largest lake in Bali, Lake Batur.

PAGES 210–211: A resident troupe of musicians, or gamelan *gong gede,* prays for inspiration at Pura Ulun Danu, Batur.

209

LEFT: Pura Ulun Danu is a complex of nine temples situated on the rim of the active volcano, Gunung Batur. Its multi-tiered *merus* were reconstructed after an eruption in 1917 engulfed the temple. Dedicated to the Goddess of Lake Batur, Dewi Danu, this subak temple controls the distribution of all irrigation water flowing from the volcano.

BOTTOM: During the odelon at Pura Besakih, the *pemangku*s bestow blessings of holy water. In the main courtyard of Pura Penataran Agung, worshippers sit before the lotus throne Tiga Sakti Padmasana. This throne symbolizes the three seats of the gods and is the focal point of ritual at Besakih.

OPPOSITE: Gusti Mangku Kulun Kulkul is the *pemangku,* or curator, of Pura Ulun, Besakih. He supervises ceremonies, receives offerings, and, during rituals, may act as the trance medium for the temple spirit.

The Balinese are fervent believers in spirits such as *butas, kalas* and *leyaks*—the witches and goblins who cast spells and cause trouble. Every village has a Pura Dalem, a temple where the deities of death are propitiated. During these rituals, the souls of deceased Balinese are elevated to a higher spiritual status. The *paduraksa* gate leading to the inner courtyard is heavily ornamented with magical *buta* and *kala* spirits.

Bali is a rare example of how an ancient culture can withstand the onslaught of the modern age yet retain its magical and intimate connection to ritual, divinity, and an artistic way of life. Despite Western commercialization, the Balinese are a traditional, animistic Hindu society. At the heart of their religion is the universal spirit of Shiva. Known to them as Siwa Raditya, the Sun God, he has danced this world into existence. Hence, they see everything as being divinely emanated. The acknowledgment of nature's absolute sacredness and the conception of time as being infinitely divided into a ceremonial calendar remind the Balinese of how every moment is a blessing and an unfolding of divine reality.

Pura Beji in Sangsit is a subak temple featuring fifteenth-century, northern-Balinese, baroque carving at its finest. Rows of pink sandstone towers mimic the Himalaya, providing thrones for the gods.

Pura Luhur is situated on the wet, forested slopes of
Gunung Batukau, the second highest peak in Bali. The
shrine is one of the Nine Directional Temples and contains a seven-tiered *meru* to Mahadevi, as well as *meru*s
honoring the deified ancestors of the royal family of
Tabanan. Everyone passing Candi Bentar, the split gate of
Pura Luhur, should be clean, pure, and properly attired in
a sarong and sash.

Every Balinese village has a Pura Desa where community ceremonies are performed. Pura Desa Gede Peliatan displays the talents of the local artisans who have carved the *raksasa*—the fierce guardians posted at the temple gates. The face over the door is *Bhoma*, a monster who darkens the moon by swallowing it.

Gunung Kawi is a massive rock-hewn memorial
shrine at the Pakerisan River Gorge near
Tampaksiring. A village elder stands before
monuments commemorating a royal family of
the Udayana Dynasty who died in the eleventh
century.

Goa Gajah is located near the Petanu River at
Peliatan. It includes the celebrated Elephant Cave,
thought to be constructed in the eleventh century
for Buddhist meditation. This large well is used for
purification rites. Six carved nymphs channel spring
water into two areas, one for men, one for women.
A small basin provides holy water.

*Pemangku*s bestow holy water upon worshipers who have come to the springs of Tirta Empul in Tampaksiring. It is said that the bubbling waters have such magical and curative powers that even the god Indra came here to find *amrita,* the drink of immortality.

OPPOSITE: Repair and decoration of the temple site is part of the extensive preparation for an odelon festival at Pura Desa Pande in Peliatan. Guardian statues in front of the *paduraksa,* or inner courtyard entrance, are wrapped in magical, checkered cloth to ward off evil spirits and unwelcome guests. The Pande clan are jewelry makers and have the privilege of forging the *kris*—the sacred dagger fashioned in the shape of a *naga.*

OPPOSITE: Demons and gods protect the entrance to Pura Meduwe Karang in the town of Singaraja on Bali's northern coast. Translating as "temple of the owner of the land," it is dedicated to dry agriculture.

Women prepare elaborate offerings of fruit, rice cakes, and flowers as a feast for the gods who will be invited by the *pedanda* to attend festivities in their honor. Pura Kehan was originally an animistic shrine that became the state temple of the Bangli Kingdom. Its eight terraces ascend the cool, forested, lower slopes of Gunung Batur.

OPPOSITE: Kulkul towers contain wooden drums used to summon worshipers for religious events. The kulkul tower at Pura Pusa Bangli is covered with ornate representations of the Balinese Hindu pantheon.

The lotus throne of Pura Kehan is upheld by the Cosmic Turtle, Bedawang Nala. Two entwining *nagas* restrain his movements, which the Balinese believe cause earthquakes.

A carved *naga* at Pura Desa Tegaltamu in Batubulan.

These rice fields near the village of Abang are are irrigated with water from the Gunung Agung volcano.

OPPOSITE TOP: Water originating from the slopes of Gunung Batukau irrigates Bimbling's vast expanse of rice fields.

OPPOSITE BOTTOM: Rice terraces extend down the Sayan Ridge to the Ayung River.

OPPOSITE: Garuda, the mythical bird and vehicle of Vishnu, stands under the roof of the *bale,* or pavilion, at Pura Desa Adat Batuan.

ABOVE: *top left,* Mahakara, or Kali incarnated as Time, Pura Dalem, Sidan; *top right,* a lotus throne or *padmasana* at Pura Sada, Kapal; *bottom left,* Gilded wooden doors of Ubud Palace, Ubud; *bottom right,* Doors of Pura Desa Adat, Batuan.

Dewi Partimawati performs the as a condong, or court attendant, in the Legong Dance of the Divine Nymph.

OPPOSITE: Although the Legong Kraton is the most feminine and refined of Balinese dances, it requires great strength and rigorous training to master the technique of its highly stylized body movements and hand gestures. The Legong is danced by three young girls, chosen as young as five-years-old for their beauty and flexibility. They train through imitation of master teachers. The most talented dancers "enter and feel" the dance.

The Legong was originally a specific narrative, but it has since become abstract. Its plot is now loosely suggested through gamelan music. The story involves a princess who is kidnapped and imprisoned by an evil king. To win her freedom, her brother wars against the king who has been warned by a crow that he will die in battle.

The condong begins the performance alone. She is then joined by two identical legongs, at which point she exits, leaving the legongs to continue the passionate dance. Moving in perfect unison, they separate into multiple characters and then reunite to complete the intricate dance pattern. The condong reappears as the crow and the three dancers whirl and dip together to the finale.

230

# GLOSSARY

Numbers in parentheses indicate page references.

**Agama Tirtha**    Balinese religion of holy water; the worship of streams, lakes, ponds, and other bodies of water    (208)

**amrita**    divine nectar, elixir of immortality    (208, 220)

**anda**    egg-shaped *lingam*, primordial shape of the universe    (61)

**apsara**    Hindu divine nymph; goddess born from the foam of the milky ocean; ideal of Khmer beauty; celestial dancer    (126–27)

**asana**    yogic position    (55, 97)

**autochthonous deity**    indigenous spirit that springs spontaneously from the landscape    (23)

**avadhuta**    state of being dispelled of all imperfections; type of yogic trance    (55)

**Avalokitesvara**    Mahayana Bodhisattva of compassion    (118)

**bakti**    Hindu devotion to a deity constituting a way to salvation    (207)

**banten**    Balinese ritual offering, often of incense, water, and prayer    (208)

**baray**    artificial lake or reservoir constructed by the Khmers in Cambodia, used to store water for irrigation during the dry season    (109)

**Bhoma**    a Balinese monster who darkens the moon by swallowing it    (217)

**bhusparsha mudra**    earth-touching ritual hand gesture symbolizing the earth bearing witness to Buddha's enlightenment (*see mudra*)    (163)

**Bodhisattva**    in Mahayana Buddhism, a being whose essence is intelligence and who is moved by compassionate zeal to postpone his or her own entrance into nirvana to help all mankind achieve enlightenment    (87, 118)

**bodhi tree**    *Ficus religiosa*, sacred fig tree, also known as the pipal or wisdom tree, under which Siddhartha became enlightened    (76, 105, 166, 169, 190)

**Bon Po**    indigenous religion of Tibet; form of pre-Buddhist nature/animistic worship presided over by shamans in Tibet, Ladakh, and Bhutan    (194)

**Brahma**    creator of the universe, represented with four faces looking in four directions; one of three gods in the Hindu trinity    (134, 207)

**Buddha**    the awakened one; an enlightened being; ninth avatar of Vishnu; son of Maya and Suddhodana, king of the Shakyas; also known as Shakya Muni, "an ascetic of the Shakya tribe" (*see* Siddhartha Gautama)    (81, 82, 105, 106, 130, 132, 138, 145, 163, 166, 169, 172, 175, 186, 198)

**chakra**    one of five ascending levels of psychic energy centers in the body, each a symbol of Dharma, the Buddhist wheel of time    (87)

**chedi**    Thai stupa    (142, 147, 149, 156, 159)

**chofa**    "sky tassel;" Thai architectural detail on rooftop edges representing the elongated neck of Garuda    (150)

**chorten**    Tibetan stupa    (80)

**condong**    court attendant in the Balinese Legong dance    (230)

**darshan**    holy sight; seeing the divine; auspicious sight    (53)

**Dharma**    the universal truth; the teachings of virtue and principle; religion; duty, law; the holy order; underlying foundation of Buddhism    (87, 106)

**Dharmadatu Jnan**    becoming one with the universe; achieving enlightenment    (82)

**Dharma wheel**    teachings of Buddha: the four noble truths and the eight-fold path    (82, 104, 106)

**dharmsala**    temple shelter for pilgrims    (60)

**digambara**    "sky-clad," naked; a description of Shiva    (55)

**dorje**    symbol of Vajrayana Buddhism; Tibetan thunderbolt symbol figured as a diamond scepter, used to control electrical, illuminating power of enlightenment    (195, 232)

**Durga**    manifestation, depicted with ten arms, of Shiva's consort Parvati, the Mother Goddess, as destroyer of demons    (63, 71)

**Ganesh**    in Hindu mythology, elephant-headed son of Shiva and Parvati; the remover of obstacles; knowledge; lord of the *ganas*    (136)

**Ganga**    in Hindu mythology, the celestial river, child of the mountains; also Mother Ganga, goddess of the Ganges River in India    (94)

**garbha**    hemispherical dome of a stupa, representing the womb and infinite dome of sky from which all is emanated; the Buddha nature    (76, 80, 87, 132)

**Garuda**    mythical Hindu deity that is part eagle, part human; enemy of the *nagas* and vehicle of Vishnu    (150, 229)

**ghat**    stone platform, usually by banks of a river, used for meditation, cremation, and other Hindu rituals    (56, 92, 101)

**gompa**    Tibetan Buddhist temple, lamasary    (194)

**Gurung**    native tribe of the Annapurna Himal, in Nepal    (29, 30, 32, 41)

**Harmika**    cone of the stupa, representing fire    (87)

**himal**    parallel group of peaks    (22, 29)

**Himalaya**    abode of snows, highest mountains in the world    (16, 17, 22, 60, 208)

**hti**    umbrella-shaped architectural element near top of a stupa; insignia of air    (87)

**Indra**  Vedic god of war and storms, depicted as a four-armed man on a white elephant, carrying a thunderbolt; drinker of soma  (220)

**jyoti**  curling finial atop a stupa; symbol of fire, ether, enlightenment  (87)

**Kailash**  world mountain; Himalayan peak in western Tibet considered the home of Shiva; the most important place of pilgrimage for Hindus and Buddhists  (17)

**Kali**  Hindu Black Goddess of destruction and death; the destroyer, all-annihilating; time; wife of Shiva  (44, 63, 71, 73, 229)

**Kamandal(u)**  water pot; one of the ritual objects carried by Shiva ascetics  (91)

**karma**  principle that every action has a consequence affecting reincarnation; action, work; an act and its results; law of cause and effect  (16, 105, 132)

**Kasi**  Varanasi, India; City of Light  (90)

**Khmer**  indigenous people of Cambodia, creators of Angkor  (109)

**kris**  Balinese sacred dagger in the shape of a snake, believed to have supernatural powers  (220)

**Legong Kraton**  most feminine and refined of Balinese dances; Dance of the Divine Nymph  (230)

**lingam**  phallus symbolizing Shiva's creative power and his potential to emanate the universe  (16, 17, 52, 53, 61, 94, 139, 153)

**longyi**  Burmese sarong or wrapped skirt  (191)

**Mahakara**  Balinese Kali incarnated as Time  (229)

**Mahaparikrama**  Hindu great pilgrimage circuit from southern India to Mount Kailash and back again  (16–17)

**Mahayana Buddhism**  "the greater vehicle;" second of two major divisions of Buddhism, as practiced in the north, e.g. China, Korea, Vietnam, Tibet, and Japan (*see* Theravada Buddhism)  (194–95, 207)

**Maitreya**  literally, "friendly and benevolent" in Sanskrit; Buddha of the Future, the coming Buddha, usually depicted as fat and laughing  (198)

**mandala**  concentric diagram of the sacred universe used for meditation; power circle  (22, 49, 130)

**mantra**  chant used in meditation and prayer; sacred syllable, word, holy name, or secret formula repeated over and over in the mind to bring calmness and focus  (94)

**mauneya unmada**  *munis* intoxication; state of ecstatic trance sensitizing and aligning seers to invisible energies emanating from the holy sites  (22)

**meru**  multitiered Balinese temple representing the holy peaks of the Himalaya; refers to Mount Meru, the world mountain  (113, 212, 216)

**moksha**  release of one's soul; liberation from karmic suffering, the ceaseless cycle of birth, death, and reincarnation, which can be achieved only through enlightenment  (94, 105)

**Mount Meru**  abode of the gods on earth; mythological center and axis of the Hindu universe, located in the Himalaya; central peak of the world; also called Sumeru  (82, 109, 182)

**mudra**  ritual hand gesture symbolizing Sanskrit alphabet characters; essential element in Buddhist iconography  (64, 87, 106, 132, 163)

**munis**  an ascetic, a yogi; a sage, as in Shakyamuni, or Sage of the Shakyas, which is another name for Buddha  (22)

**naga**  serpent deity that controls water and all treasures beneath the earth; symbol of water, rain, and the monsoon, and of fertility and riches  (74, 76, 113, 114, 123, 159, 220, 225)

**Nandi**  a bull, Shiva's mount, said to have been given to him by Brahma as a reward for settling a dispute; symbol of happiness and strength  (63)

**nat**  one of 37 pre-Buddhist, animistic deities worshiped by the Burmese  (166, 185)

**Newar**  native tribe of the Kathmandu Valley, Nepal  (48, 52, 73)

**nirvana**  state of an empty or still mind; extinction of self; enlightenment; achievement of perfect wisdom and compassion resulting in freedom from rebirth; highest spiritual goal of Hindus and Buddhists  (87, 105, 130)

**Padmasambhava**  the great guru who brought Mahayana Buddhism to Ladakh and Tibet in the 7th or 8th century  (44, 195)

**padmasana**  the lotus throne, with ritual seats for the Hindu trinity of Brahma, Vishnu, and Shiva  (207, 229)

**paduraksa**  inner courtyard entrance of a Balinese temple  (214, 220)

**pedanda**  Balinese priest  (208, 223)

**pemangku**  Balinese priest  (212, 220)

**phar phum**  Thai spirit house; miniature temple found in homes, workplaces, and public areas  (147)

**phi**  pre-Buddhist animistic spirits; foundation of Thai beliefs  (147)

**pindu**  mark representing the Third Eye, or Wisdom Eye, of Shiva  (65)

**pradakshina**  clockwise circumambulation around a stupa while repeating a mantra, a ritual through which energy is created; reenacts turning of the Dharma wheel  (169)

**prang**  Khmer-style temple spire representing Meru  (156)

**prasad**  sacred offering to the gods; gift  (208)

**prayag**  sacred confluence of waters; place of sacrifice and spiritual power and object of pilgrimage  (23, 71, 93, 208)

**psychocosmogram**  architectural representation of the cosmos; physical "map" to enlightenment  (87)

**puja**  Hindu worship such as prayer, ringing of a bell, a rice offering, anointing with milk, butter, or holy water  (17, 61, 80, 207)

**raksasa**   Hindu demons and fiends   (217)

**Ramayana**   Hindu epic of Rama and Sita   (73, 139)

**rudraksha**   rosary of beads made from seeds of the utrasum (*Elaeocarpus*) tree   (68)

**sadhu**   Shiva ascetic, wandering renunciant; holy man, yogi   (16, 49, 52, 55, 56, 64, 65, 91, 101, 102)

**sadhvi**   female Shiva ascetic   (55)

**samadh**   being buried alive, a yogic austerity   (56)

**samsara**   ceaseless cycle of birth, death, and reincarnation   (94)

**sannyasi**   seeker, wandering ascetic, one who has control of his senses; Hindu holy man   (16, 55, 68, 105)

**Shiva**   god of destruction and renewal; procreator of the universe; master of dance; the divine yogi; god of the ascetics; one of three deities in the Hindu holy trinity   (53, 55, 63, 64, 68, 73, 94, 134, 156, 182, 207)

**Siddhartha Gautama**   historical prince of the Shakya clan, son of Suddhodana and Maya, born in Lumbini, Nepal, c. 490 B.C., died c. 410 B.C. according to recent research (dates may vary widely depending on sources); upon achieving enlightenment, became the Buddha   (49, 74, 76, 82, 90, 104, 105)

**sikhara**   temple spire representing a Himalayan holy peak   (186)

**sphatika**   crystal rosary worn by Agori *sadhus*   (102)

**stupa**   dome-shaped funereal monument, a reliquary containing the remains of great teachers and religious leaders; symbol of Buddhist enlightenment   (81, 82, 83, 132, 169, 170, 182, 185)

**subak temple**   Balinese temple of rice cultivation and water distribution   (209, 215)

**Swayambhu**   "The Self Created;" a sacred site where Vipaswi, an ascetic, threw a lotus root into a lake where it bloomed into a flower of a thousand petals and emanated a magnificent light   (74, 75)

**Tantric Buddhism**   esoteric branch of Buddhism incorporating aspects of Samkya yoga and Vajrayana Buddhism   (48, 87, 203, 207)

**tapas**   bodily heat; concentrated yogic energy; fervor, ardor   (64)

**tapasya**   one who practices austerities, or self-inflicted suffering, to gain psychic powers and control over the physical body   (55, 64)

**tathagata garbha**   suchness, thatness; "thus come from the womb;" that which is beyond differentiation; state from which all reality is manifested; the Buddha nature   (132)

**thanaka**   traditional Burmese cosmetic made from jasmine and sandalwood paste   (190)

**Theravada Buddhism**   "the lesser vehicle;" original, conservative branch of Buddhism, as practiced in the south, e.g. Sri Lanka, Myanmar, Thailand, Laos, and Cambodia (*see* Mahayana Buddhism)   (150, 179)

**tirtha**   river crossing, ford; place of pilgrimage and purification   (96)

**tirtha yatra**   physical act of fording a river or stream; undertaking a journey to a sacred confluence of water; ancient tradition of pilgrimage to holy places   (23, 97)

**tilaks**   painted body marks of Shiva *sadhus*   (65)

**tonyas**   Balinese animistic nature spirits residing in certain trees   (209)

**Trisakti**   Balinese Hindu trinity of gods who create, uphold, and destroy the universe   (207)

**urdhvalinga**   erect *lingam* symbolizing creation and yogic control over the physical senses   (73)

**vahana**   vehicle; creature or being that represents a particular god's energy or character   (63)

**vajra**   thunderbolt; diamond scepter; symbolic tool used to control the electrical, illuminating power of Buddhist enlightenment; symbol of the absolute   (195, 232)

**Vajrayana Buddhism**   resultant joining of Mahayana Buddhism and the ancient animistic religion of Bon Po; religion of Tibet, Bhutan, and parts of Nepal   (48, 192, 195 203)

**vibhuti**   holy ash representing Shiva's dissolution of the universe, the end of the eternal cosmic cycle   (55)

**virtakas**   passionless state; chasteness, yogic control of sexuality; one of the vows of a Hindu ascetic   (73)

**Vishnu**   supreme god; preserver, protector, and dreamer of the world; second in the Hindu trinity   (52, 60, 109, 113, 134, 207, 229)

**wat**   Thai Buddhist temple   (145, 147, 153, 156, 159, 163)

**Yama**   god of the underworld, who judges and punishes souls; represented as green, four-armed being seated on a buffalo and clad in garments of fire   (122)

**yadna**   Balinese ritual worship   (207)

**yantra**   sacred geometrical design usually of intersecting triangles, representing levels of consciousness and used for meditation   (embossed on cover)

**yogin**   Hindu renunciant who practices yoga; spiritual master; ascetic   (17, 55, 56, 97)

**yuga**   one of four Hindu time, or age, cycles of the world; names of each are derived from the four throws of the dice: *krita, treta, dvapara,* and *kali*   (74)

**yoga**   strict spiritual discipline undertaken to gain control of the mind and body in order to achieve nirvana; to yoke, join together, harness   (55)

# INDEX

Dedicated to MARTHA McGUIRE, the one I love,
who walked by my side every step of the way.

# ACKNOWLEDGMENTS

Deep gratitude to those special editors who typed, rewrote text, and helped select images: My family—Martha McGuire and Richard Ortner; and brilliant friends—Mary Kalamaras, who devoted her energy and talents to the project; Neal Goldsmith, who accompanied me on my first trip to the Himalaya; and Kevin Buckley, for his special editorial contribution to the original story, *Where Every Breath is a Prayer*, which appeared in *GEO* magazine.

Many thanks to those who believed in my work and made this book possible: Lena Tabori, Nai Chang, Linda Sunshine, Wendy Burton, Alice Wong, and all of the rest of the dedicated, talented staff at STC.

Thank you Stan Melancon, for teaching me about Hinduism and sharing a passion for the Himalaya; Judith Chase, for your hospitality in Kathmandu; Professor A. Verdu, for your inspired instruction in Eastern philosophy; and Wayne Herndon, for your generous friendship and encouragement.

Thanks to RBR Color Lab, New York, NY; Jerry Grossman, Nikon Inc.; Barry Tannenbaum, *Nikon World* magazine; and Elisabeth Biondi, editor of *GEO* magazine, for my two features on the Himalaya.

Great appreciation and respect are due to all the erudite holy men, *sadhus*, monks, priests, and *pedandas* who shared their knowledge, gave access into the inner sanctums of temples, and extended extraordinary hospitality and interest in this project.

My thanks to the talented dance troupes who participated: The Royal Institute for Nepali Sacred Arts, Kathmandu, Nepal; Cultural Academy of Leh, Ladakh, India; The Old Chiang Mai Cultural Center, Chiang Mai, Thailand; Royal Classical Yogyanese Dance Company, Yogyakarta, Java; The Gatilan Dancers, Prambanan, Java; and Semara Ratih, Ubud, Bali.

Thanks also to those intrepid guides, translators, drivers, boatmen, cooks, and the many Sherpa, Gurung, and Tamang porters, who carried tons of gear, especially: Ang Tsering Sherpa of Seti, Nepal and Pemba Tsering Sherpa of Thami, Nepal; Jivan of Kathmandu; Leang Chay of Siem Reap, Cambodia; Mur of Yogyakarta, Java; Nyoman Moding of Ubud, Bali; Ravi of Kedar Ghat and Shyam Ji Pandit of Varanasi, India; and all those whose warm hospitality we enjoyed.

And finally, thanks to my loving parents, Anne and Archie, whose encouragement allowed me to grow and follow my heart.

Photographs of Amaranath ice *lingam* on page 16 courtesy of Mahatta of Srinager, India. Debossed image on front cover: Borobudur mandala, courtesy, Yazir Marzuki, Pt Penerbit Djambatan, Jakarta, Indonesia. Excerpt on page 16 from *Siddhartha* by Herman Hesse. Copyright ©1951 by New Directions Publishing Corp. Reprinted by permission of New Directions Publishing Corp; for the United Kingdom, permission granted by Gerald Pollinger Ltd., London, England.

Photographs and text © 1996 Jon Ortner
Foreword © 1996 Bill Kurtis
Preface © 1996 John Sanday

Published in 2001 by Abbeville Press.
All rights reserved under international copyright conventions.
No part of this book may be reproduced or utilized in any form or by
any means, electronic or mechanical, including photocopying, recording,
or by any information storage and retrieval system, without permission
in writing from the publisher.
Inquiries should be addressed to Abbeville Publishing Group,
22 Cortlandt Street, New York, N.Y. 10007.
Printed and bound in Japan.

First published in 1996 by Stewart, Tabori & Chang.

Library of Congress Cataloguing-in-Publication Data

Ortner, Jon, 1951–
Sacred places of Asia : Where every breath is a prayer / Jon Ortner.
p. cm.
Rev. ed. of: Where every breath is a prayer. 1996.
ISBN 0-7892-0705-2
1. Shrines—Asia, South—Pictorial works. 2. Sacred space—Asia,
South—Pictorial works. 3. Shrines—Asia, Southeastern—Pictorial works.
4. Sacred space—Asia, Southeastern—Pictorial works.  I. Title: Where every
breath is a prayer. II. Ortner, Jon, 1951 - Where every breath is a prayer.
III. Title.

BL 1055.076 2001
291.3'5'095—dc21                          00-065012

Edited by Mary Kalamaras
Designed by Nai Y. Chang
Production by Louise Kurtz

10   9   8   7   6   5   4   3   2   1

First edition

FRONT COVER: *Sadhu* on the Ganges River Varanasi, India.

OPENING: A Sukhothai-style Buddha from Wat Phan Tao, Chiang Mai, Thailand.

PAGE 2: *top,* Ama Dablam Peak, Khumbu, Nepal. More than 22,000 feet high, Ama Dablam is sacred to the Sherpas of eastern Nepal; *bottom,* Ananda Temple, Bagan, Myanmar.

PAGE 3: *top,* Bayon Temple in Angkor Wat, Cambodia; *bottom,* Machapuchare, Annapurna Himal, central Nepal.

PAGE 4: *top left,* Kangtega Peak, Khumbu, Nepal; *top right,* Shwedagon Pagoda, Yangon Myanmar; *middle left,* Dhammayangyi Temple, Bagan, Myanmar; *middle right,* Dhaulagiri Peak, Central Nepal; *bottom left,* Mount Everest, Khumbu, Nepal; *bottom right,* Wat Benjamabopit, Bangkok, Thailand.

PAGE 5: Sunrise on the Ganges River, Varanasi, India.

PAGE 6: *top,* The Shiva temple Gedong Songo on the conifer-covered slopes of Mount Ungaran on the Dieng Plateau, Java; *bottom,* Himlung Himal taken from the Duna Khola, Nepal.

PAGE 7: *top,* Phungi Peak, Manaslu Himal, Nepal; *bottom,* Pandra Shivalaya, or The Fifteen Abodes in Pashupati, Kathmandu, Nepal.

PAGE 18-19: The Nilgiri Himal, rising above the eastern wall of the Kali Gandaki Gorge in Nepal.

PAGE 20-21: Bejeweled guardians uphold a Mon-style *chedi,* or "golden mountain," on the upper terrace of Wat Phra Kaeo temple compound in Bangkok, Thailand.

BACK COVER: Nun on Maha Aung Mye Bosan Monastery, Inwa, Myanmar.

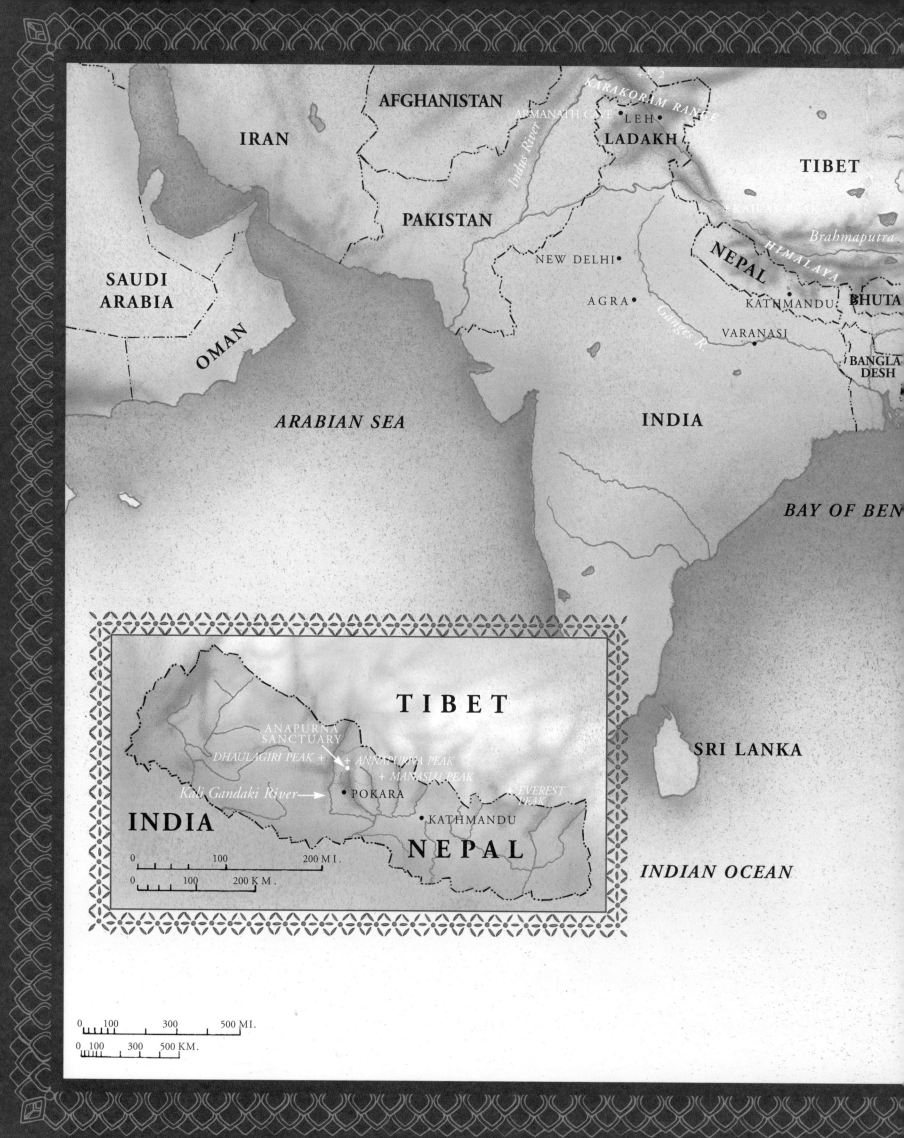

AFGHANISTAN

IRAN

SAUDI
ARABIA

OMAN

PAKISTAN

*Indus River*

AMARNATH CAVE
LEH
LADAKH

KARAKORAM RANGE

+ K 2

TIBET

+ KAILAS PEAK

*Brahmaputra*

NEPAL

HIMALAYA

KATHMANDU
BHUTAN

NEW DELHI

AGRA

*Ganges R.*

VARANASI

BANGLA
DESH

ARABIAN SEA

INDIA

BAY OF BEN

SRI LANKA

TIBET

ANAPURNA
SANCTUARY

DHAULAGIRI PEAK +

+ ANNAPURNA PEAK
+ MANASLU PEAK

*Kali Gandaki River*

• POKARA

EVEREST
PEAK

INDIA

• KATHMANDU

NEPAL

0          100          200 MI.

0     100     200 K.M.

INDIAN OCEAN

0    100      300          500 MI.

0  100      300    500 KM.